REQUIEM FOR YUGOSLAVIA

Borka Tomljenović

Printed in Ann Arbor, Michigan.

Designed and typeset by Codex Productions, Inc.
2581 Burton Rd., Ann Arbor, MI 48104

Contents

List of Photographs

Acknowledgements

I WISH TO acknowledge my debt to John V.A. Fine Jr., Professor at the Department of History, University of Michigan, and to Benjamin Stolz, Professor at the Department of Slavonic Languages, University of Michigan, for kindly reading my manuscript, and suggesting a number of corrections and improvements.

I wish to thank John Hamer of Codex Productions, Inc. for typesetting my manuscript and preparing it for print.

My warm thanks go to my daughter, Katarina T. Borer. Without her constant help and support this book could never have been published.

Preface

REQUIEM FOR YUGOSLAVIA was written three years after I had left war torn Yugoslavia, in 1992, and settled in the USA. It represents my farewell to the country in which I was born and lived seven decades. It expresses my deep grief over the demise of my former homeland, most of which has now become a foreign country for me. I am thus taking an emotional leave of Yugoslavia as a unified country.

I was born in a multiethnic Bosnia, at the end of World War I, then still part of the Austro-Hungary, married a Croat and for 25 years lived in Croatia, while the subsequent 25 years I spent in Belgrade. Thus, I had lived in three different parts of Yugoslavia long enough to have become quite familiar with the peculiar cultural climate that prevailed in each of them, and to become fond of each for different reasons. For me, until very recently all of Yugoslavia was my homeland, and I viewed the ethnic and cultural diversity that existed in various parts of the country as a rich heritage that belonged to all of us, regardless of ethnic and religious distinctions. Recent disintegration of Yugoslavia and the war that followed it have prompted me to think about the reasons that have brought about its collapse.

Yugoslavia was an artificially created country that came into being after World War I. It was made up of Croatia, Slovenia, Dalmatia, and Bosnia and Hercegovina, which were set free after the downfall of Austro-Hungary, and of Serbia and Montenegro, which at the time were sovereign states. In this manner, the newly created country has combined cultural traditions from the east and those from the west, traditions which have in the past met and clashed in these regions, but never quite merged. Until 1918 the parts of which Yugoslavia was made had followed very different and distinct historical paths. They were separated both by their religion and by the historical circumstances that shaped their culture and character. It was, therefore, not surprising that there should be misunderstandings and tensions when they were brought together in a common state, which eventually led to the collapse of the country. To me, such approach provides a clue to the conflicts that have torn apart and devastated my former homeland.

In June 1991 my daughter, and her son and husband traveled with me across some parts of what then still was Yugoslavia. We visited Serbian medieval monasteries, beautiful towns along the Dalmatian coast, and ended our tour in the Baroque Zagreb. During this brief journey we were able to perceive a great diversity in cultural heritage that each of the visited parts of Yugoslavia displayed. When a year later I immigrated to USA, I began to think that this journey could serve as a basis for a book – a travelogue in which I could write about my lost country, about its natural beauty as well as about its rich and diverse cultural heritage.

During the next 3 years, however, Yugoslavia ceased to exist as a unified and ethnically diverse country. A number of dissident states emerged, and my native Bosnia, which represents Yugoslavia in miniature, was plunged into a fratricidal war. I was receiving letters from my friends both from Zagreb and from Belgrade, and to a great extent they reflect their thoughts and reactions to the course the events had taken in former Yugoslavia. I used these letters to form a new section of the book which is entitled Broken Connections. It is a kind of a running commentary on current events, while at the same time reflecting the differences that separate the two main protagonists, Serbs from Croats. At the same time these letters disclose the extent of the psychological trauma that the ethnic desintegration and the war have created.

Three years later, in June 1994, my daughter and I revisited our former homeland, Zagreb and Opatija, and then Belgrade. This last section of the book, which I have called Epitaphs, provided me with an opportunity to record how people felt and what they thought about the newly created situation. It also evoked nostalgic memories of the time when I lived in those parts of now divided Yugoslavia. These episodes shed light on the characteristics that distinguish and separate one part of the country from the other, and Serbs from Croats, the differences that have eventually led to the desintegration of Yugoslavia.

It is my hope that my book will find its way to a wide range of readers – to the Americans of Yugoslav origin, to the students and those who are interested in the history and culture of Yugoslavia, and not the least to those who may wish to travel there once peace has settled down again in my former homeland.

Ann Arbor, June 1995 B.T.

BYZANTIUM

Byzantium

In the first half of June 1991 we travelled for the last time through some parts of what was still Yugoslavia. Our plan was to visit medieval monasteries and churches in Serbia and Kosovo, and then drive along the Montenegrin and Dalmatian Littorals to visit several of the ancient towns on the Adriatic coast before ending our trip in Zagreb.

Our little party included my daughter, Katarina, her younger son, Richard, her husband, Paul, and me. Each of us sought something special and different in this tour. My daughter, who had suggested the trip, had long wanted to see the Serbian medieval monasteries and their frescoes that she had heard so much about. For my American-born grandson it was an opportunity to see many of the historical and cultural treasures of Yugoslavia which he had never seen. My son-in-law was looking forward to touring Yugoslavia with "natives", and for me, it was a chance to visit the cradle of Serbian history and part of my heritage, to revisit the beautiful Dalmatian coast with which I associate some of my dearest memories, and once more to see Zagreb, where I had spent the most meaningful years of my life.

In this way we travelled through Serbia, Montenegro, and Croatia, three of the six Yugoslav republics, the remaining three being Slovenia, Bosnia and Hercegovina, and Macedonia.

At the time of our tour Yugoslavia was not yet at war but some disturbing signs indicated the approaching conflict. We could not, however, have anticipated the tragic course of events that was soon to lead to the disintegration of the country and the terrible bloodshed that this event was to precipitate. We did not realize at the time that this journey was to be a farewell to the old Yugoslavia.

From Belgrade,we set out on our journey looking forward to the pleasures associated with travelling and sightseeing. Our first stop was to be at Manasija, near Kraljevo. As the lovely countryside we were passing through looked so attractive we agreed that it would be a good idea to have our lunch somewhere in the open first. We chose a pleasant-looking place by the road only to discover at closer inspection that it was part of an old cemetery. Undeterred, we sat down in the shade of some chestnut trees, but when we opened our picnic basket we found out that we had forgotten our delicious sandwiches in Belgrade. We consoled ourselves with some dry biscuits and then walked a little about the cemetery. My non-Orthodox family listened with great interest as I told them about some of the customs connected with the cult of the dead observed by our people. At funerals, food is brought to the grave and shared by all who join the mourners, and some of it is left behind, apparently for the beggars. Another and probably more credible explanation of this custom is provided by ethnologists, who see it as an offering to the deceased person and to dead ancestors, a custom which goes back to pre-Christian times. People go on observing such customs long after their true meaning and the reason for observing them have been lost and forgotten.

The cult of the dead is very much alive with the Orthodox Serbs, and is manifested in many different ways. One such moving way of showing respect for the memory of the dead person is the custom of erecting roadside stone memorials. Most of these are dedicated to the soldiers killed during the Balkan and the First World Wars. In a naive and vivid style the figure of the dead man is portrayed in an army uniform with a rifle at his side, and the text on the back of such a memorial tells the passer-by his sad story. Serbian history is a long account of struggles for independence and wars waged in defense of freedom.

Our first stop was Manasija, the 15th century fortress-monastery near Kraljevo, built by Despot Stefan Lazarević at the time when the Serbian state had already become a vassal to the Turkish conquerors. As the Turks advanced into the Balkans the defeated Serbs were obliged to move the centers of their medieval state away from the dangerous south to the north. Our route from north to south led us, therefore, backwards into the past, from the relatively more recent towards the oldest Serbian monasteries, which date from the 12th century.

The most important churches and monasteries were built during the rule of the Nemanjić dynasty, which ruled from the 12th to the late 14th century, and they represent three distinct schools of Serbian church architecture, the Raška, the Morava, and the Serbian-Byzantine schools.

The Raška school, the oldest and the most Serbian of the three schools, with representative monuments dating from the late twelfth and thirteenth century, is a synthesis of Western and local traditions. With its blind arcades and sculptured human, animal and vegetable decorations around the portals and windows these churches reveal a strong Romanesque influence. The principal churches of the Raška school are Studenica (1209), Mileševa (1237), and Sopoćani (1265), all built of stone, often of highly polished marble.

The Morava style can be found in the monuments in the area of the West and the Great Morava rivers, built in the 14th and 15th centuries; this style combines local traditions with influences coming from as far away as Macedonia, the Adriatic coast, and Mount Athos in Greece. Most of the churches of the Morava school are built of alternating layers of stone and brick. The facades are distinguished by decorative elements in the shape of a chess board and sculptured bas-relief decorations. Ravanica (1381) is a good example of the Morava school.

The Serbo-Byzantine school, limited to the southern parts of medieval Serbia, close to Byzantine territory, expresses to a greater extent characteristics of Eastern traditions, with a profusion of domes, cupolas and arches, and very little external sculpting. Alternate layers of colored bricks and stone decorate the facades of these churches producing a very exotic and distinctly oriental effect. Graćanica (1320) is a good example of the Serbo-Byzantine school of architecture.

Manasija

Manasija (1407-8) is representative of the Morava school and is considered to have been one of the most elegant buildings in medieval Serbia. High stone walls with 11 towers surround and protect the church, which stands amidst a beautifully groomed garden. The ruins of the former scriptorium - the writing school, of Despot Stefan Lazarević -, reminds us that this was still a place of learning and a cultural center before the Serbian state finally disappeared under the Ottomans.

Manasija (1407-8)

The frescoes depicting graceful figures with dreamy expressions, looking very poetic and gentle, are painted in shades of azure, blue and gold. Particularly notable among them are the Entry into Jerusalem, the scenes of Christ's miracles, the Assumption of the Virgin on the west wall, and the figures of the warrior saints, a frequent theme in Serbian medieval fresco painting. These holy warriors at Manasija, so representative of Despot Stefan's court, are a last farewell from the Balkans before being overpowered by

Ravanica (1370-1389)

the Turks, for Manasija is the last major religious monument of medieval Serbia. My feeling of sadness was soon dispelled by a group of chattering and noisy schoolchildren spilling out of a bus, who had come to pay a visit to this ancient monastery.

Ravanica

We next stopped at Ravanica, close to Ćuprija, the endowment of Prince Lazar (1370-1389), built just before the

Ravanica, Orthodox nuns

Battle of Kosovo in 1389. After his heroic death at this fateful battle, he was canonized and buried in Ravanica. This monastery was frequently ravaged during the Turkish period , and in 1690 its monks joined the Patriarch Arsenije Čarnojević, who led a migration of 70,000 Serbs north into the Vojvodina. The relics of Prince Lazar were laid to rest in a small church they built near St.Andreja, at the heart of the new settlement. The remains of Prince Lazar were to be moved twice more, first to the Vrdnik monastery in Fruška

Gora, and eventually to the partly ruined Ravanica. Fruška Gora, a small mountain near the Danube not higher than 539 m was called Mons almus,beneficial,salutary mountain, by the Romans who are credited with having introduced wine-growing there. Ravanica had several subsequent restorations, including the contemporary one, which have restored it its former guise. Built of alternate layers of brick and stone, with its chequered ornaments of red and yellow chess boards, Ravanica looked gay and bright by comparison to the sober and austere Manasija.

Today Ravanica is a nunnery, as is the case with the majority of our monasteries, but in the past most of them, like those in Greece, were exclusively male enclaves. Repression of the church under the communist regime, confiscation of church properties, and persecution including the execution of many Orthodox priests by the Croatian Ustaše during World War II, contributed to the gradual takeover of Serbian monasteries by the nuns.

We were received by two Orthodox nuns, dressed in black medieval habits, with cylindrical black kamilavka caps on their heads. As living representations of the images on the frescos covering the walls of our monasteries, the two nuns eager to show us their church fussed unsuccessfully to unlock the door with an ancient key before finally accepting the American technical expertise provided by my son-in-law. The frescoes had been badly damaged, but those

Žiča (1196-1228), Mother superior

that were spared had been painted in fluid lines and light colors. Particularly memorable were the finely modelled figures of Knez Lazar, the founder of the church, his wife Princess Milica, and their two sons, Stefan and Vukan. Other remarkable frescoes are Christ's Entry into Jerusalem, and the Healing of the Blind in the south choir and the figures of the holy warriors.

Žiča

The monastery of Žiča, near Kraljevo, was next. It is the endowment of King Stefan,the First-Crowned (1196-1228) and dates back to the early 13th century.

When we arrived at Žiča we found part of the church under scaffolding and a lot of reconstruction work going on. Frequently ravaged in its long history, sacked both by the Turks and Bulgarians, and bombed during World War II, Žiča now has been restored almost to its former glory.

Dedicated to the Ascension, Žiča examplifies the mature Raška school of architecture. Its frescoes date from different periods, the oldest from the time of St.Savo are in a very poor, faded state of preservation and resemble those from the Studenica monastery. The holy warriors on the southern wall and the large depiction of the Assumption on the northern wall are notable examples of 14th century painting. The frescoes depicting the theme of the Christmas Hymn above the west door at the entrance of the church are of great artistic beauty and value.

The monastery complex, encircled by walls, includes several other buildings, among them the konak, the nuns' quarters.

In terms of historical and artistic importance Žiča is among the most valuable monuments of medieval Serbia. This is where Stefan Prvovjenćani was crowned, and St.Savo established autocephalous bishopric of the Serbian Orthodox church.

King Stefan, the First-Crowned, was the son of Stefan Nemanja, the founder of the Nemanjić dynasty of Serbian medieval kings. King Stefan for a time broke his ties with Byzantium and turned to the west, to Venice and Rome,to seek help against the invading Hungarians and Bulgarians. He received a crown from Rome, from Pope Honorius III,

Žiča, Jacob's Ladder

who sought to convert him to Catholicism. Stefan, in the end, did not forsake his Orthodoxy thanks to the influence of his younger brother Rastko, who had become a monk, and assumed the name of Savo. Thanks to him the Serbian Church was elevated to the status of an autocephalous archbishopric, and the monastery of Žiča became the episcopal seat. This event sealed the destiny of the Serbs, for it solidified its ties with Eastern Orthodoxy. It influenced the course of Serbian history and provided the basis for later conflicts, persecutions by and confrontations with the South Slavs who embraced Occidental Christianity. Today, we can only speculate what the history of Serbian people might have looked like had Stefan the First Crowned embraced Catholicism together with the crown from the Pope. Thus, Žiča played a vital part in Serbian history. Today,like most other Serbian monasteries, Žiča is a nunnery.

After we had seen the church, we paid a visit to the Mother Superior, the Igumanija Justina. We were received in the new and very modern konak, the nuns' quarters, a building full of light and sunshine and potted flowers.

We wanted to see the examples of the recent school of icon painting, an ancient art that had fallen into oblivion but has recently been reestablished at Žiča and several other monasteries. Igumanija Justina graciously complied with our wish, and took us to the studio, a large and light room with a row of windows looking onto a lovely garden. Several nuns, in their black habits and kamilavkas, were sitting at their benches bent over the icons they were in the process of painting. Igumanija Justina introduced us to one of them and left us there after making us promise to take a cup of coffee with her when our visit was over.

Ever since I had first heard of this new school of icon painting, I had made up my mind to obtain an icon painted there for my youngest grandson, Richard. Now that we actually were on the spot, it was exciting to walk about the studio in the company of my grandson looking at the exhibited icons. Our choice fell on the same icon, St.Jacob's Ladder, painted after the beautiful fresco in the Virgin Perivlepta church in Ohrid.

While drinking Turkish coffee with Mother Justina, we talked over the details of the purchase of the icon we had chosen. A very bright young nun, Sister Makrina, was in charge of the business side of the talk. Her mind worked like a calculator, and she had no difficulty in converting deutchmarks into dollars and back. We agreed on the price of $1000 for the icon, but did not think twice about the sum, for it was to be painted on a specially treated piece of linden wood, lovely, exotic, and at once both an object of art, and of tradition.

We left $100 deposit; no written receipts were given or asked for. It was agreed that the icon would be delivered to me in the monastery of Vavedenje in Belgrade, about a year later; true to their word, a year later I received it.

Maglič, the medieval castle in the Ibar valley

Studenica

We left Žiča and drove along the densely forested river Ibar. Our next destination was Studenica, near Ušće on the Ibar river. We caught a glimpse of the stately Maglič fortress, perched high above the river, one of the most beautiful and best preserved medieval castles in Serbia. There was not much traffic on the road and on approaching Studenica we ran across a large flock of sheep grazing by the road. This pastoral scene was a fitting prelude to our visit to this an-

Studenica (1168-1196), King's church

cient monastery. We passed along a grove of yellow acacias, in full bloom. They reminded me of a romantic story about lilac trees I heard when I first visited Studenica with my

Studenica, Portal to the Mother of God's Church

Studenica, Mother of God's Church, Crucifixion

sister many years ago. These lilacs are associated with a Serbian queen, Jelena of Anjou, who in the 13th century married King Uroš I. Legend has it that he ordered lilac trees to be planted along the road leading to Studenica in her honor. In this gallant and romantic way King Uroš welcomed her arrival in her new homeland. Regretfully, there was not much evidence of these old lilac trees.

It was raining when we arrived at Studenica, entering the monastery through an immense wooden door and gate-

Studenica, fresco of King Milutin (1282-1321)

way within an ancient and strong stone wall with ramparts and towers. Inside was a complex of several sacral buildings, built at different periods. The central place is occupied by Studenica, a church dedicated to the Mother of God, Bogorodičina crkva. It was built in the 12th century, as an endowment of Stefan Nemanja (1168-1196), the founder of Serbia's medieval dynasty of kings. Studenica is the resting place of Stefan Nemanja and his wife Anastasija, their sons Vukan and Stefan, and a number of other Nemanjić family members as well as other dignitaries.

Studenica, built of polished stone, with Romanesque portals and windows decorated with fantastically sculptured animals, human figures and plants, is one of the finest churches in the style of the Raška school. The church is of lofty proportions and is richly decorated with frescoes dat-

Studenica, King's Church, Presentation in the Temple

ing from different periods. The oldest, from the 13th century, were painted on the gilt and blue background reminescent of mosaics, with a magnificent Crucifixion on the west wall. Some of the frescoes, vandalized in the past, had had their figures defaced with chisels which left white marks on them. These white marks produce an effect of a snowstorm in which the figures on the frescoes had been caught.

Radoslav's narthex, added in the 13th century, has fragments of frescoes with portraits of the Nemanjić dynasty.

Its treasury contains a few objects from Stefan Nemanja's time, most notably a gold ring belonging to Stefan the First-Crowned. Among the other valuables there is the 14th-century cover for the coffin of Stefan the First-Crowned, em-

Studenica, King's Church, Birth of the Virgin

broidered by Olivera, the daughter of Prince Lazar and later wife of the Turkish Sultan Bayazid I.

The King's church, Kraljeva crkva, was designed on a much smaller and more modest scale. It is a fine example of the cruciform plan, so characteristic of Orthodox churches. It was built in the 13th century by King Milutin, who became known as "an indefatigable builder of divine churches".

Orthodox churches display some characteristics that distinguish them from other Christian churches. They are often built on a round or square plan and are surmounted by cupolas and domes. The altar in the apse, is separated from the main body of the church by a high screen, the iconostasis, decorated with icons. There are no seats in an Orthodox church; the congregation stands during the interminable service. But the most distinctive feature of a

Serbian medieval church are its frescoes. These frescoes reflect well the time and the society in which they were created. Frescoes were as durable as mosaics and also less expensive. They were painted on walls which were first covered with several layers of plaster, usually four, and then, after the penultimate one was dry, the painter would trace a rough outline of the intended work upon it. The final coat of plaster was then applied and the pigment was painted straight on while the plaster was still wet and absorbent. Frescoes were a much more spontaneous medium than the more rigid mosaics.

The frescoes in the King's church are imbued with classical beauty. Outstanding among them are the Presentation of the Virgin in the Temple on the north wall and in particular the moving scene of the Nativity of the Virgin on the south wall. Fine details, like the testing of the water in the font by the hand of one of the women in preparation for the bathing of the infant, makes this fresco very human and gives it a universal quality. There are also portraits of King Milutin and his fourth wife, Simonida, of St.Savo, and of Stefan Nemanja.

We took a look at the recently restored dining-hall, a huge room with rows upon rows of stone benches and tables, where monks once took their meals during which another monk was supposed to read to them from the lectern passages from the Scriptures. There was also a big fire place to keep them warm on cold winter days. It all had an authentic monastic atmosphere; the only trouble was that there were not enough monks nowadays to fill those benches.

On the long verandah of the monks' quarters we were greeted by Abbot Sava, the Archimandrite of the monastery. He warmly pressed us to have lunch with him, which we gladly accepted, being quite exhausted after all the sightseeng. During the meal Abbot Sava showed keen interest in my son-in-law, who comes from a Mennonite family. Orthodox and Protestant churches have always shown interest in each other, the common bond being, no doubt, their repudiation of the Roman Pope. We enjoyed the lenten, but deliciously prepared food, brought in by a nun, who also waited upon us all through the meal.

Sopoćani

After we left Studenica, we drove along the Ibar valley until early in the evening we entered Kosovo on our way to Sopoćani in the vicinity of Novi Pazar. We had difficulty in finding a place to put up for the night in Novi Pazar, a town very oriental in character. Eventually, we had to go to a place outside the town, a kind of hostel and apparently the property of some business organization. It was in a somewhat isolated place, but from the outside looked inviting enough. When we were shown the rooms and told that there was only one bathroom and toilet for the whole building,

Sopoćani (1242-76) view from the Lipa Hostel

our enthusiasm tapered off. However, we were consoled on discovering quite unexpectedly that from the window of that bathroom, if one were actually standing in the tub, one had a lovely view of austere Sopoćani nestling like a white dove inside a green nest of the dark forest.

There was not much evidence of any other guests in the Lipa hostel, but when we unpacked and came downstairs for our dinner in the little garden, we saw some young

Sopoćani, Dormition of the Mother of God

people sitting at a table a little apart. Visitors from Novi Pazar? The place had a peculiar, almost uncanny atmosphere, and my grandson Richard diagnosed it as a suitable setting for one of Agatha Christi's mystery novels.

For dinner we were faced with a menu that you can expect all over Yugoslavia - massive meat dishes but few vegetables or salad. For a change we decided on cottage cheese with "kajmak", rich cream, and our tea was tasteless and lukewarm.

Our waiter and the manager of the Lipa was a young and efficient Albanian. The Albanians are a hard-working and thrifty people, ready to do all sorts of manual work. They have developed a chain of confectioner's shops all over Yugoslavia in which they sell pastry and specialities like "burek", meat pie. They are also eager buyers of land and houses because they always have ready cash.

The following morning we went on foot to pay our visit to Sopoćani, also famous for its frescoes. The church was built on a lonely but very beautiful site. Standing amidst fields and meadows and gently rolling hills it gives the impression of a somewhat desolate and neglected monastery. In the past it was badly devastated and for many centuries stood like a ruin, without a roof to protect its precious frescoes, until it was reasonably well restored in the 20th century. The tower and the exonarthex, added by Tsar Dušan, still stand uncovered, and the walls surrounding the church have fallen into neglect.

Dedicated to the Trinity, the church was built in the 13th century by King Uroš I.(1243 - 1276), and is the resting place of the founder, whose body is kept in a stone sarcophagus, and of his mother, Ann Dandolo, the granddaughter of the Venetian Doge Enrico Dandolo. The church displays strong Romanesque characteristics with blind arcades and doors and windows built of stone and sculptured with animal, vegetable and human decorations. The inside of the church impressed me with its austere simplicity as did much of the exterior. The large surfaces of its walls readily lent themselves to monumental compositions, well-known for their exceptional harmony of colors and disposition of groups of angels and apostles. The figures in the monumental fresco of the Assumption, surrounding the bier with the body of Virgin Mary, and Christ holding a swaddled baby representing the departed soul of the Virgin, have been inspired by classical ideals. The lines of their bodies are clearly recognizable under the elegantly draped robes, the movements and postures of their bodies and gestures as well as their features reveal human feelings of sustained sorrow and of respect. The whole composition radiates harmony of color with shades of green and violet, and green and pink predominating on the yellow-golden background. We felt that we were in the presence of art at its best. Because of these frescoes Sopoćani has been declared a world cultural heritage and is under the protection of the United Nations.

We spent the greater part of the morning admiring the frescoes, the Nativity with its shepherds, the holy Warriors, and many others. We reluctantly left the church but tarried a little while outside where everything was strangely quiet, in perfect harmony with the atmosphere prevailing in the church. There was no sign of human or animal presence, only a strange-looking King's fountain in the shape of a stone pillar with a huge, carved cross. The place had a peculiar charm in its utter isolation, which reminded me of Manasija, and I was overcome by the same feeling of sadness.

Before leaving this enchanted spot we wanted to call on the nuns in their quarters, a brand new building at a short distance from the church. One of the nuns came out to greet us. I asked her if they had any honey to sell, as I had espied a few bee-hives in their garden. She agreed somewhat reluctantly and we waited for a long time for her to return from the cellar with a small jar of honey. It felt cool and was of golden color, and I, being fond of honey, was very pleased to leave Sopoćani with that sweet trophy.

We are now in Kosovo proper, the part of Yugoslavia so fiercely contested between the Serbs and the far more numerous ethnic Albanians. The Serbs, outnumbered today by the Albanians, are attached to this land with strong historical and emotional ties. The churches and monasteries built here in the past by Serbian kings and noblemen today silently bear witness to their presence in these parts through long centuries.

Ss. Peter and Paul's Church

In Novi Pazar we went to see Ss. Peter and Paul's church, one of the oldest churches on Yugoslav soil. It stands on a small hill above the road to Raška, and its rustic appearance reminded me of St. Donat's church in Zadar, also built of rough stone and roughly its contemporary (9th century). Sv.Savo and Stefan the First-Crowned, Stefan Nemanja's biographers, mention that it was in this church that Stefan Nemanja converted from the Catholic to the Orthodox church. Of a quatrefoil ground plan the church is surmounted by a large dome, inside the church rests on four massive pilasters. Fragments of frescoes from different peri-

Ss. Peter and Paul's (9th cent.), interior

ods survive in unequal state of preservation. Some of them go among the oldest medieval Serbian frescoes known. A cemetery around the church displays tilted stone crosses of a peculiar shape. The place looked sad and abandoned, we got the key to the church, of an extraordinary size, from a woman living in a house nearby. She acts as a custodian to this ancient church which does not seem to be a place of worship any more today.

Ss. Peter and Paul's, fresco of St. John the Baptist

Novi Pazar with minarets and mosques, which give it a strong oriental character, looks almost like some town in the Near East. This impression became even more apparent when we reached Priština, the capital of the Kosovo autonomous region. Few women could be seen in the streets while men were very much in evidence. Our car with a foreign licence plate immediately attracted the attention of an Albanian who offered his services to change our Dollars for Dinars at a rate higher than in the bank. We thought to

Priština, Kosovo, a Moslem woman

have struck a good deal only to realize a moment later that an other dealer was offering more. We soon came to recognize each other, the Albanian dealers had pockets bulging with worthless Dinars, and we looked so obviously out of this place. My grandson was very amused with this half-secret activity carried on so openly in the street. For him many things looked strange, and some he saw for the first time in his life. Like the oxcart we encountered on the highway leading to Priština, or a woman wearing dimije, a garb worn by Moslem women.

Gračanica

We left Priština, and on our way to Gračanica we had a picnic lunch on a field by the road, a very pleasant respite from our loaded sightseeing schedule. Soon, we reached

Gračanica, known to be one of the best examples of the churches built in the Serbian-Byzantine style.

Gračanica is one of the most beautiful and best preserved monuments of Serbian medieval architecture. As we entered through the big gate the graceful arches and vaults of Gračanica, rising one upon another towards the central cupola left a powerful impression of a well-balanced movement upwards. It comes as a sudden surprise behind a high wall that surrounds the monastery. A flock of sheep was peacefully grazing in the churchyard, and several pillars dating from the Roman time completed this serene summer scene. We were told by a woman who was in charge that the sisters were all out mowing the grass in the field. So she offered to take us round the church as a guide.

Gračanica was built in the 14th century by King Milutin, and at one time it served as a cathedral church, today it stands like an islet surrounded by an unfriendly sea.

The frescoes date from different periods, some are of arresting beauty like the ascetic figure of St.John the Baptist, or the charming scene of St.Elija in the cave fed by a raven. The portraits of King Milutin and his young wife Simonida, as well as of King Uroš and his wife Jelena of Anjou, King Konstantin and Queen Jelena are full of dignity and beauty.

King Milutin has the reputation of the Serbian Henry VIII for he, too, changed wives several times, but did not

Gračanica (cca 1315)

get rid of them in exactely the same way as Henry VIII. He married and dismissed them for political reasons. Jelena, the first wife, was the daughter of the sebastocrator Jovan, a high state dignitary, and was sent back home when Milutin found it more opportune to marry Jelisaveta, the daughter of the Hungarian King Stefan V. Soon enough, she suffered a similar fate and was succeeded by the daughter of the Bulgarian Tsar Terterije I. She, too, was sent back to her family when Milutin was obliged to come to terms with Byzantium and

Gračanica, fresco Mother of God with Child

when he married Simonida, the 5-year-old daughter of Byzantine king Andronicus II. Her elegant figure in the Gračanica inspired our poet Milan Rakić (1876 - 1938) to write a sonnet in her honor. In it he speaks of her blinded eyes ascribing this barbaric act to an Albanian, who had stealthily scraped them out of the fresco with a knife. A more likely explanation could be found in the superstitious belief of credulous people that the powder from the eyes scraped from frescoes has a healing and miracle-working power.

We left Priština and drove on to Peć to visit "the Tall Dečani" and the Peć Patriarchate, our last leg before reaching the Adriatic coast. Along the way we spotted a gypsy camp by the road with the man of the family quietly smoking by an open fire, and with a tent and a cart nearby. These fiercely independent nomads of our time can still be seen

Gypsy camp in Kosovo

with their caravans and tents in some parts of our country. It was more than 30 years ago that I had seen such a Gypsy caravan when traveling here with Joan Scrutton, an English friend of mine. Like then, these Gypsies were sitting round the fire on which their meal was cooking, while their horses were grazing close by. A big, shabby-looking bear, a constant member of a Gypsy camp, was tied up to the carriage, meekly bearing his unenviable lot. I remember seeing such bears led by their Gypsy masters through the streets of Belgrade on the occasion of some state holidays. When their masters provided some music on their violins and drums the poor animal tethered with a nose ring would stand on its rear feet and perform a pathetic dance. This show attracted some donations from spectators both in the street and from the windows. The gypsies we encountered on our way seemed to be still following their traditional way of living, but nowadays it is not unusual to see Gypsies travelling in a car instead of in their caravan.

The High Dečani

We reached Dečani late in the afternoon approaching it down a shady lane. A large flock of sheep with clappers ringing temporarily blocked our path. The impact this church makes upon you is very strong because you do not expect to find a church of such proportions in so remote and isolated a place. Serbian kings, however, liked to build their monasteries and churches in remote sites of outstanding beauty. This church is surrounded with densely wooded mountains.

Dečani, the biggest, cathedral, church of medieval Serbia, is one of the glories of its architecture. It was built in Raška style of polished marble slabs and it is the most lav-

To Dečani

Dečani, Trifora

ishly decorated church in our country. The Romanesque, Gothic and Byzantine elements have been perfectly and elegantly blended in this church, which captures you by the quiet harmony of its proportions.

Dečani is the endowment of King Stefan III, who was named after it Stefan Dečanski. It was built in the first half of the 14th century and its architect was "Fra Vita, of the order of Franciscan friars, the master builder from Kotor, the city of kings", as it is stated in the inscription engraved in the architrave of the northern portal. The windows, biforas and triforas, and the portals are all richly sculptured with fantastic zoomorphic and vegetable decorations. I particularly liked the sculptured detail of Christ's baptism above the entrance gate of the church. Inside the church there are over 1000 frescoes, the largest number among all Serbian

Dečani (1321-1331)

monasteries. These frescoes, however, cannot bear comparison with those from the 13th century, from the time of King Milutin.

Of the special documentary value are the portraits of historic personages, as seen in the detailed family tree of the Nemanjić dynasty, in which are included almost all the members of this famous family of Serbian kings. Despite frequent looting and ravages in its past, after 600 years Dečani is still beautifully preserved.

Dečani, Portal

Sarcophagus with the body of King Stefan Dečanski brought back to my mind an event from 1959 during my first visit to these parts of my country in the company of my English friend. We were studying the frescoes in this church when a young Albanian Moslem woman, accompanied with her two small children, entered the church. She approached the sarcophagus and placed on it a few cobs of corn and some squashes as offerings, then she crouched and crawled under it and made her children do the same. A young monk

Dečani, the Nemanjić Family Tree

who was accompanying my friend and me told us that the local Albanian population from the village of Dečani had taken the church under their protection during the last war, and that in general they hold this place in high esteem and pay it every respect. They believe in the miracle-working powers of the dead king, and such scenes as we had then witnessed were quite frequent.

In the Middle Ages these parts were mostly populated by Serbs, but after the big Migrations of Serbs to Vojvodina

Mileševa (cca 1234-36)

in the 17th and the first half of the 18th century, they became inhabited by the Albanian settlers from the northern Albania and they became majority population.

I remember some of the stories and traditions associated with Dečani as they were told us by that young monk many years ago. He told us that the two huge bees-wax candles, that can still be seen on each side of the imperial gates of the altar, had been given as a present to the church by Princess Milica after the tragic battle of Kosovo in 1389, when Serbian army was defeated by much stronger Turks. Those candles were to be lighted, centuries later, by the avenger of Kosovo. The grandioze, bronze chandelier, decorated with two-headed eagles and with griffons and other fantastic creatures, was also a present of Princess Milica and of her son Despot Stefan Lazarević (Despot was the title of

The White Angel on Christ's Tomb

Serbian rulers after the Battle of Kosovo). The legend has it that this chandelier was made from the arms of the Serbian noblemen fallen in the Battle of Kosovo. And he told us that the glittering bits of metal that could be seen in the circle on the floor in front of the altar are the remains of the former rich, gold decorations, which had been removed and taken away by the Bulgarian soldiers during the Balkan Wars.

Such thoughts and memories crossed my mind as 33 years later once again I gazed at that 600 years old church. From today's perspective it is difficult to believe that once it was the center of Serbian culture and spirituality.

Mileševa

We spent about two days in Peć while visiting Dečani and the Peć Patriarchate, staying at a very modern and new hotel, called Metohija. It was quite comfortable, and from

The Peć Patriarchate (13th cent.)

the large terrace to which we had access from our rooms, we could look at the menacing and austere peaks of the Rugovo Gorge, which separated us from the Adriatic and its Mediteranean culture. My grandson and I spent some time wandering around the city and looking at its bazaar-like shops in search of some presents. We did not have to walk too long before we came upon a small but very neat shop. Its Albanian owner sold home-woven carpets of all sizes and other goods made of wool. There my daughter chose a very nice medium sized carpet in traditional colors and patterns, known as the Pirot design. Richard, my grandson, on the other hand was delighted to buy several hand-woven bags, but I did not buy anything. At my age I have learnt to resist such temptations.

My daughter and her husband planned to visit the 13th century Mileševa monastery near Prijepolje, the pleasure I could not afford because only one afternoon was left for this

The Peć Patriarchate, Dormition of the Virgin, Holy Warriors

tiring expedition. The monastery was hard to reach, but well-worth the effort for among its frescoes is the famous White Angel. Mileševa is also the place where Mehmed - paša Sokolović (1505 - 1579), the Grand Vizier of the Ottoman Empire, once went to school as a child. He was among the Serbian children abducted at regular intervals by Turks, a tribute known as the "danak u krvi", a tribute in blood. Most of them were trained to be fanatical soldiers - the Janissary, but Mehmed paša Sokolović rose to the rank of the Grand Vizier, the highest position in Turkish government. His en-

Čakor Pass

dowment is the bridge over the Drina, which he had built remembering his roots, the story told by our Nobel Prize winner, Ivo Andrić.

My daughter told me that they were disappointed by the stubborn prohibition against their taking photographies of the frescoes by a young priest caretaker. Beside the White Angel on Christ's tomb, the Virgin Mary with a distaff from the Annunciation is among other outstanding frescoes from Mileševa.

So, while they were away admiring the famous White Angel,and the place where Mehmed paša Sokolović, the grand vizier, once went to school as a child, Richard and I stayed at the hotel, in its lovely back garden overlooking the rushing Bistrica river. We sipped our tea there amid blossoming rose bushes and were quite happy to enjoy a restful afternoon.

Canyon of the Morača

We had all of our meals at this hotel, and we were waited upon by a big fellow of the headwaiter, who seemed to be all the time a little drunk. When he first came to offer us the menu and take our orders, without much ado he sat down at our table, and talked to us in an overtly friendly manner. He did not mean to be disrespectful, I think it was his way of showing that he liked us and that he had taken us under his wing. His familiarity perhaps reflected an attitude prevalent in this part of our country, which is far removed from European standards and ways of behaviour. Alas, there was always some reason to complain to him, either about the service or food, and when we did so, he would listen to us with a concerned expression on his face accompanied by frequent "tsts,ts-ts" remarks, to show his surprise and disapproval. In spite of that, things went on very much as before.

The Peć Patriarchate

We paid a brief visit to the nearby Peć Patriarchate, once the seat of Serbian Orthodox Church and the center of political and religious resistence against the Turkish oppression. It is a complex of 3 medieval churches , attached to each other, the oldest dating from the 13th century. Like other Serbian churches, they were frequently devastated and restored over the years. There were a large number of interesting frescoes to be seen, but by now we had become so satiated with all the frescoes seen in the course of our short tour, that we could feel little interest and even less pleasure in looking at the Patriarchate frescoes.

The following day we left Peć and drove to Rožaje, crossing the Prokletije mountain range, bound in ice and snow, along the romantic and wild canyons of the Lim river, and of the Morača river with turquoise blue and clear waters, and steep forested slopes alternating with cliffs. We passed 30 tunnels on our way to Titograd, and eventually reached Kotor on the Montenegrin Littoral. When still high up in the mountains we caught a glimpse of our sapphire blue Adriatic, and our spirits rose at the sight of it.

RENAISSANCE

Kotor

WE HAD A brief stop at Kotor, just enough for my daughter and son-in-law to visit its cathedral, dedicated to St. Triphon (1166), and for Richie and me to drink an espresso and write some cards at an open-air cafe there. It was good to be surrounded with palm and cypres trees and to bask in the balmy Mediterranean climate.

Then we drove off at full speed in order to reach the same evening the prince of the Adriatic – Dubrovnik. It was exciting to see the walls of this ancient city, which arose so many memories in my heart. And I could not help but think how different were the destinies of Serbia on the one hand and of Croatia on the other. How different was the world of the medieval Serbian monasteries and churches that we had just left behind from the Mediterranean world into which we have now come. To be on the Adriatic coast meant to enter a sunny and gay Mediterranean world leaving behind us the austere and meditative world of Orthodox monasteries and sad and brooding churches and frescoes of medieval

The Bay of Kotor

Serbia. To have passed in one day three geographic and climatic zones - from the Continental in Peć through the Alpine into the Montenegrin mountains, and into the Mediterranean as we reached the sea, vividly brought home to us the great differences that separate the closed, contemplative and tragic world of medieval Serbia from the exuberant and Renaissance world of sunny Dalmatia and the Mediterranean. We were passing through a sunlit landscape of slender cypress, palm, and fir trees, through "the land where lemons blossom", and where the houses are built of stone, which gives them a peculiar charm and beauty. And where in cafes facing stone-flagged squares people exchange daily gossip and news and idle away their time in the benevolent climate of the Adriatic coast.

Kotor

It was not difficult to understand and to explain the contrast between the culture of Serbia and Dalmatia as a consequence of historical circumstances. Unlike medieval Serbia, Mediterranean Dalmatia was not in the way of the militant and invading Ottomans. By conquereing Serbia the Turks interrupted and retarded its development for five centuries, influencing greatly the way of life and the character of people. Even though the Turks threatened and endangered Europe they never remained long enough to leave lasting marks there, except for the now so popular coffee, which was unknown in Europe until the Turks were defeated at Vienna (1683), and for the Viennese crescent rolls that have been commemorating the victory over the Turkish crescent moon ever since. Dalmatia has always been part of the civilized Mediterranean world, and the history of its people was shaped and influenced by Venice, the Habsburgs, and briefly even by the French during the Napoleonic wars, who all belonged to the western cultural circle. One is almost tempted to think that the geographical position of a country is the most decisive factor in its history. Thus, the Serbs, in their past closely connected with and influenced by Byzantium, and later under the Ottomans, and the Croats under the Habsburgs and Venice, developed for centuries separately under the influence of two essentially very different cultures. Later on in my life, I was frequently reminded of what I had heard from our history master, Rade Jovanović. I gave it little thought at the time, but for some reason it has stuck to my mind. He spoke of an invisible line that from Roman times on has separated the eastern part from the western part of our country, which in the course of time became representative of two essentially different cultures. This accounts for the very significant differences between them, with the language and a common Slav ancestry as the only common bonds.

Dalmatia

While we were traveling through Serbia and Kosovo we did not come across any open signs of disorder or unrest nor did we actually anticipate any. Only once was our car stopped on the road by the police who were puzzled by the fact that we did not have plates on both ends of our car.

The Roofs of Dubrovnik

They had never seen such a car before. But as we drove along the Adriatic highway we were struck by a lack of traffic. We hardly met any cars as we drove at full speed towards Dubrovnik on an almost deserted highway. This time of year the traffic on the Adriatic highway is usually lively with the cars of both domestic and foreign tourists. Only once, at Zaton near Dubrovnik, did we encounter a car with some French people with whom I exchanged a few words. They told me that they had been coming for many years to the Dalmatian Coast and expressed their concern about the problems our country was at the time coping with.

Dubrovnik

The feeling of isolation and loneliness grew even stronger as we reached Dubrovnik. The manager of the half-

A Side Street in Dubrovnik

empty Bellevue Hotel, a new establishment I was not familiar with, appeared quite depressed and pessimistic about the outcome of the season. And with good reason, for when we went out to take a walk in the lovely streets of Dubrovnik, instead of an international crowd of all kinds of tourists we encountered only a small group of French tourists. If there were any other tourists there they were not in evidence in the practically deserted streets of Dubrovnik. As we entered the narrow side streets full of small, picturesque restaurants, known for their local specialities, we were solicited, pressed and importuned from all sides by their owners who were eagerly watching out for customers. Some of them even followed us for a distance, and almost all of them offered free wine if we decided to dine at their place.

My associations with Dubrovnik go way back. As a child I vacationed there with my mother and sister. We had stayed at the somewhat secluded Lapad Hotel and I remember candle-lit dinners in the garden accompanied by the discreet music of a small orchestra. In those days, before World War II, Dubrovnik was still an exclusive resort, visited by well-to-do families, many of them from Sarajevo and Belgrade. After the war things very much changed, and this peaceful city of former noble families became a first class tourist attraction. This has brought money and prosperity but it has also robbed the town of its former gentility.

Its past glory is still very much evident in the unique beauty of the city walls and the other monuments that grace the town. While the rest of Dalmatia was ruled by Venice and Austria the small city-republic of Ragusa – Dubrovnik – protected its freedom and its independence by promoting commerce. Its merchants traveled inland to Bosnia and Serbia, while its ships, "argosies", were frequent visitors at the ports all over the Mediterranean and the Near East. Ragusans are known to have had a colony in 16th century London. Dubrovnik can boast of having enriched the English language with the word argosy, a word that was used by Shakespeare in his plays. In the past Dubrovnik was known under the name of Ragusa, and in 16th century

England it was referred to as Aragouse. Hence the name for the ships from that town.

The prosperity that commerce brought in its wake created a good climate for the cultural development of the city, which gave birth to numerous scientists, like the 16th century mathematician Marin Getaldić (1568-1626), and the 18th century philosopher and astronomer Rudjer Bošković (1711-1787), and to a great many poets, like Ivan Gundulić (1589-1638), and playwrights, some of whom, like Marin Držić (1508-1567), have remained popular to this day. In his comedies Držić has truthfully brought to life characters of the 16th century Dubrovnik, and the servant Pomet from the comedy Dundo Maroje (Uncle Maroye) actually anticipated Beaumarchais's Figaro.

From my former visits to Dubrovnik and its environs I have retained an interesting memory, which throws some light on its past. One summer shortly after the World War II my parents spent their summer holidays on the small island of Lopud, and they invited me and their granddaughter Rina to join them there. Lopud is very near Dubrovnik, and in the past many noble families from Dubrovnik had their summer residences on that island. A small church dedicated to Our Lady of Šunj, Gospa od Šunja, is situated in a secluded cove, and to reach it you had to pass through an old olive and fig grove. A charming walk to take, and there I directed my steps one afternoon in search of things and

Clock Tower and the Sponza Palace

times long forgotten. While walking about the church my attention was soon captured by a strange-looking life-size wooden sculpture of the 12 apostles. I was so intrigued and impressed by their obviously foreign appearance that I decided to look for a priest or some other person who might be able to provide a clue to the origin of this mysterious group of apostles. It was the sacristan who eventually told me that according to the local tradition the apostles were brought from England in the 16th century by a Ragusan merchant who happened to be there with his ship, argosy, at the time Henry VIII outlawed the monasteries. That Ragusan merchant apparently found the sculpture abandoned on a heap of rubbish, and he dutifully transferred it to his argosy and safely brought it home and donated it to the Church of Our Lady of Šunj.

The name of the English King Richard the Lion Hearted is also connected with Dubrovnik. During his ill-fated return from the campain against the Saracens in Palestine he was caught in a storm in the Adriatic. He made a vow, if he remained alive, to build a church on the spot where he touched land. He landed on the small island of Lokrum, near Dubrovnik. In Dubrovnik King Richard was given such a warm welcome that he felt obliged to build the church in Dubrovnik instead of on the island of Lokrum. The church was one of the most beautiful in Dalmatia, and served as the cathedral church, until it was completely destroyed by the earthquake in 1667. The visit of King Richard to Dubrovnik in 1192, though recorded in most of the old chronicles, could not be historically corroborated.

One could spend months in exploring and admiring the sights and the beauty of Dubrovnik, but we could stay there only three days, for we were anxious to visit some other places on the Adriatic Coast and to stay for a little while in Zagreb at the end of our journey. What sightseeing we did was mostly due to my daughter and her husband. They went

Orlando's Column (1419), and the Cathedral

on their own exploring the town at random, while Richard and I relaxed at the Gradska kavana - City cafe. It would be difficult to do full justice to all the treasures that Dubrovnik possess, and it would be equally difficult to make a fair selection from among so much wealth and beauty.

A good point to start from, however, is the Pile Gate, one of several gates leading into the walled medieval city. As you cross the small wooden bridge you are greeted by St. Blaise (Sveti Vlaho),the city's patron saint, who gazes upon you from a niche above the gate with a model of the city in his hands. Such statues will be seen in many other places of the city. Once you have passed through the gate you find yourself on the Stradun, the stone flagged street with stone houses on both sides and the Clock tower at the end. You will see the lovely,round Onofrio Fountain, dating from the 15th century and facing it the 14th century Franciscan monastery (Male braće) with the moving sculpture of the Pieta above the entrance door. Inside, there is a lovely garden full of flowers and an old cistern, surrounded with a graceful colonade. The place is fraught with an atmosphere that invites one to contemplation. The monastery has the third oldest pharmacy in Europe in operation since 1391, with a small collection of ancient medical instruments. At the other end of the Stradun stands the Clock Tower with two bronze medieval soldiers, called Zelenkos, holding mallets with which they strike hours. Close by is the Sponza palace, in former days the customs house, and St. Blaise'a Baroque church opposite it. On the small square between them stands the Orlando Column (1419), a medieval knight who bears the Dubrovnik banner, and is the symbol of its freedom. Orlando (Roland) was a historic figure from the 8th century, who lost his life in the Pyrenees when returning from a military action against the Saracens in Spain. He served as a model for an ideal knight in the medieval cycle of poems about Charlemagne. Orlando's statue in Dubrovnik

Rector's Palace

is associated with the following legend. Orlando, who was Charlemagne's nephew and the governor in Brittany, heard that Saracens had raided Roman cities on the Adriatic, including Dubrovnik. He immediately boarded a Ragusan ship, an argosy, and came to Dubrovnik where he won victory over Saracen pirates. The grateful citizens, later on, had a marble statue of Orlando erected to commemorate the event. The actual statue of Orlando was made in 1418 by the local sculptor, Antun Dubrovčanin, Antun from Dubrovnik. Today, Orlando statue is a place specially favoured by local pigeons and foreign tourists, who like to have their pictures taken in front of him. One of the treasures of Dubrovnik is the Rector's Palace from the 15th century, in the Gothic style with Renaissance elements added later on. Once, it was the seat of the Rector of the Republic,

Sedan chair of the Saraca Family

but today it has been turned into a museum, and part of it houses the archives with the numerous and valuable documents related to the past of the Republic and its relations with the world. Very impressive are the material remains from the past in the form of furniture and such intriguing objects as the sedan-chairs belonging to former noble families bearing their coats-of-arms. Dubrovnik was an aristocratic republic and commoners were barred from public affairs. Nevertheless, its statutes were very democratic, and the Rector served without remuneration. The inscription in the Rector's Palace admonishes:

Oblite privatorum – publicae curate
(Relinquish private affairs –
and concern yourself with the public cause.)

Close to the Ploče Gate, at the southern end of the walls, is the Dominican monastery, dating from 14th century. A mixture of Gothic and Romanesque elements lends a particular charm to its architecture. In its neighbourhood is the old "Lazaret", quarantine hospital, where once passengers had to spend some time before being admitted into the town, for fear of contagious diseases. Today it serves as a lively market place.

Hvar, Petar Hektorović's Tvrdalj

Hvar

A ferry-boat at Drvenik conveyed our car over to the island of Hvar, the ancient Pharos, famous for its mild climate in winter, and the plantations of lavender, among which we were soon driving to Stari Grad.

This detour was principally motivated by our desire to visit Tvrdalj castle. Tvrdalj was built in the 16th century by Petar Hektorović, (1487-1572) a Croatian Renaissance poet and Latin scholar. Already during his lifetime Hektorović was renowned for his translation of Ovid, the third such translation of that Roman poet ever, and a testimony to Hektorovic's erudition in the spirit of classical culture. He recognized the value and the beauty of our folk poetry almost three centuries before the Romantic Revival, when folk poetry began to be appreciated by poets like Goethe, Byron, Pushkin and Merime.

In his work "Ribanje i ribarsko prigovaranje" (Fishing and Fishermen's Talk), he described in a simple and realistic manner the three days he spent fishing between Stari Grad on the island of Hvar and the islands of Brač and Šolta in the company of two fishermen from Hvar, Paskoje and Nikola. He faithfully recorded his conversation with these two simple and illiterate fishermen, who entertained him by singing folk songs. Hektorović was so struck by their beauty that he wrote down some of them, including two long epic poems known as "bugarštice", popular ballads describing tragic events from our past. He recorded not only the actual words he had heard from the fishermen, but also their melodies, using standard musical notation. One bugarštica was about Prince Marko and his brother Andrijaš, the other about Prince Marko and Radoje Severinac. Prince Marko was a central figure in our folk poetry from the period of the Ottoman rule, who fought against the injustice and tyranny of the Turkish masters. Hektorović reports that the two fishermen sang "in the old manner", i.e. the manner long established and practiced, they sang their songs "in Serbian style", "as they always did among themselves".

Thus, Petar Hektorović was one of the precursors of those poets who later on in the 18th and 19th centuries discovered the value and beauty of folk poetry and became its champions, which Hektorović was quick to notice two centuries earlier.

The Western and Mediterranean parts of our country, which were under the rule of Austria, Hungary and Venice, enjoyed continuity in spiritual and literary creativity while at the same time the central and eastern parts, under the Turkish rule, suffered from a period of stagnation. The circumstances that contributed to the growth of the literary language and written literature differed from the circumstances that stimulated the growth of oral literature. However, it was precisely in those regions, which did not feel the beneficial influence of the Renaissance movement from the west that the oral folk literature developed and reached its highest level of perfection. It was brought about not only because of specific historical circumstances but also because of the rich spiritual heritage, which became preserved in oral poetry.

THE DEATH OF THE MOTHER OF THE JUGOVIĆI

What a wonderful sight, oh God, it was
When the warriors rallied on the Field of Blackbirds.
The nine Jugovići brothers were in the army,
And old Jug-Bogdan was the tenth among them.

The Mother of the Jugovići prays to God
To give her falcon's eyes,

And a swan's white wings,
So that she might fly to the Field of Blackbirds
And see the nine Jugovići brothers.

What she asked for, God granted her,
He gave her falcon's eyes,
And a swan's white wings,
And she flew to the broad Field of Blackbirds.

There she found dead the nine Jugovići
And old Jug-Bogdan among them.
Above them stood nine battle lances,
On the lances sat nine falcons,
Round the lances stood nine good horses,
And beside them nine fierce lions.

Then the nine good horses began to whinny,
And the nine fierce lions to roar,
And the nine falcons to scream.

But the Mother had hardened her heart,
And did not shed a tear.

She takes the nine good horses,
And she takes the nine fierce lions,
And she takes the nine falcons,
And returns with them to her white mansion.

Her daughters-in-law saw her from afar,
And walked out to meet her.
Then the nine widows began to wail,
And the nine orphans began to cry,
The nine good horses began to whinny,
And the nine fierce lions to roar,
And the nine falcons to scream.

But the Mother had hardened her heart,
And did not shed a tear.

When it was in the middle of the night,
Damian's dappled horse began to whinny.
The Mother asked Damian's wife:
My daughter-in-law, Damian's wife,
Why is Damian's dappled horse whinnying?

Is he hungry for white wheat,
Or is he thirsty for water from the Zvečan?

Damian's wife replied thus:
He is neither hungry for white wheat,
Nor is he thirsty for water from the Zvečan,
But Damian had accustomed him
To eat wheat until midnight,
And from midnight to set out with him on a journey,
He is now grieving for his master,
That he did not carry him back home.

But the Mother had hardened her heart,
And did not shed a tear.

When daybreak came in the morning,
Two black ravens were flying,
Their wings were bloodstained to the shoulders,
And white foam was around their beaks.

They were carrying the arm of a warrior,
With a gold wedding ring on the finger.
They threw the arm into the Mother's lap.

The Jugović Mother took up the arm,
And turned it over and over,

Finally she called Damian's wife:
"My daughter-in-law, Damian's wife,
Could you recognize this arm ?"

Damian's wife spoke thus:
Oh, my Mother-in-law and Damian's mother,
This is the arm of our Damian,
I recognize the gold wedding ring, Mother,
It was with me on our wedding day.
The Mother took up Damian's arm,
And turned it over and over,
And softly spoke to the arm:

Oh, my arm, my green apple,
Where did you grow, where were you plucked?
You grew up on my lap,
And you were torn off on the Field of Blackbirds.

The Mother grieved so much
That she died of a broken heart
For her nine Jugovići sons
And the old Jug-Bogdan.

Note. The Field of Blackbirds Battle, the Battle of Kosovo, is an event of paramount importance in the history of the Serbs. There in 1389 the Serbian army, led by Prince Lazar, was defeated by the much stronger Turkish forces, led by Sultan Murad. Both rulers, including the flower of Serbian nobility, lost their lives at the Battle of Kosovo. The Battle marks the beginning of a five-century stagnation in Serbian culture under alien Moslem rule of the Ottoman Turks. The Battle of Kosovo provided a

Hvar, fish pond inside Tvdalj

basis for the cycle of poems in which the collective memory of the people found expression, describing the events that preceded the battle, the battle itself, and the main protagonists involved in it. These poems, sung by wandering singers, "guslars", to the accompaniment of a simple string instrument, "gusle", spoke of the past glory of Serbian people, and of the feats and deeds of their popular heroes , and in this manner sustained the self-esteem and hope of our oppressed people.

Hektorović's castle, Tvrdalj, built in the 16th century, is still in a good state of preservation. After more than three centuries it still serves as a home to several families, some among them claiming to be Hektorović's descendants. It bears witness to the generosity of this great writer who had it built as a protection against the Turkish danger not only for himself and his family, but for his friends and neighbors as well, as stated on the stone above the gate leading to the fish-pond :

Petrus Hectoreus Marini
Filius proprio sumptu et industria
Ad suum et amicorum usus
construxit
(Petar Hektorović, the son of Marin, sparing no expense and effort, had this house built for himself and for his friends).

This as well as the inscriptions *Pro itinerantibus* (for travellers), and *Pro pauperibus* (for the poor) that stood on the house built for that purpose on the eastern part of Tvrdalj, speak eloquently about Petar Hektorović and his views on the world and its people.

His philosophy of life is reflected yet in another inscription:

Respice quod salvant nec opes
Nec gloria mundi
Non decor aut aetas mors
Quia cuncta rapit
(Know that neither riches
nor world fame nor beauty
or age can save you
For death seizes everything)

Or the one reminding us of the impermanency of human life:

Heu fugiunt fluxu
Non redeunte dies
(Alas, days are fleeing away
never to return).

We took a walk in the somewhat neglected and solitary garden with profusion of rosebushes in bloom. A stone pool framed with arcades provided a mixture of fresh and sea water to supply Hektorović and his friends with plentiful fish.

A little curiosity is perhaps the lavatory, a rarity for the Europe of his time, which he had built in the atrium next to the entrence gate with the wise inscription

Si te nosti cur superbis

(If you know yourself, why should you give yourself airs).

A small ethnographic collection , consisting of original utensils and other objects used in a Dalmatian kitchen and in the "konoba" on the island of Hvar, is exhibited inside the Tvrdalj castle.

There is a big fire-place with a hood (napa), a small millstone with two round stones for grinding of wheat and grain, a trough - a wooden vessel for preparing bread -, a "peka" (a metal cover under which bread is baked), copper vessels for keeping water, and a larger copper vessel for boiling laundry in lye. A curious objects made of copper in the shape of plate with a cover and provided with a long handle, in which live coals were carried to warm beds in winter, is known as "skaldalet" in the local dialict. There are several such "skaldalets" in the collection and they are apparently still used by some people in Dalmatia.

The "konoba" is the gound floor area in a Dalmatian house which serves as a store room to keep all kinds of utensils and tools necessary in the daily life of a farmer.

The konoba in this collection also exhibits an old wood press, "turanj", for grape pressing (such presses are still in current use on the island of Hvar). In the corner stands an old mortar gun, which was used to fire at clouds in order to disperse them and prevent hail. Such mortars were placed on elevated points of the hills which protect the valleys with vineyards, and they had been in use since 1885 following the Tyrolean fashion.

The kitchen and the konoba displayed at Tvrdalj are typical of the life style from the time of the great Croatian poet, which in its forms have not changed much on the island of Hvar up to the present day.

Split

We continued our journey, and the farther we went along the Adriatic Coast the stronger was the evidence of the national euphoria of the Croats. Almost every house had hoisted a Croat national flag, and in Split, always a stronghold of Croat nationalism, at every street corner we encountered vendors of paper flags and metal badges displaying the chessboard coat-of-arms, the insignia and symbol of Croatian identity and independence.

Split, marketplace, 1991

We stayed in Split long enough to renew our food supply at the local market, which is next to the walls of Diocletian's palace. The durability of the monumental remains of the former residence that the Roman Emperor Diocletian, built in the 4th century A.D., are still impressive and moving in spite of the decay inflicted by time and man. The palace, where Diocletian spent his last days, is the greatest Roman ruin in Eastern Europe. When in the 18th century the English architect Robert Adams visited Split,

Diocletian's Palace

then under the Venetian rule, he was so impressed by the beauty and harmony of the palace that he made a series of drawings. These drawings inspired him later on to redesign whole sections of London, Bath and Bristol in what was to become known as Georgian style, based on the principles of harmony, grace, and symetry that marked Diocletian's palace. In the course of time the palace has gone through many metamorphoses. New, Slav, settlers began to build their homes within it, and only a few original parts of the palace have survived to this day. The Peristyle is an airy rectangle with graceful arcades, the Emperor's mausoleum was turned into the cathedral in the 7th century, and the small temple into a baptistry. The 13th century Croat sculptor, Buvina, made a magnificently carved door for the cathedral, decorated with scenes from Christ's life, and others from the everyday life of Buvina's time.

Split is a hub for railway, maritime, and air traffic and is therefore full of passengers who seem to be in a hurry to get somewhere else. This gives a peculiar, and to my mind not very attractive, character to this otherwise very interesting place. I have often been in Split either waiting for a ferry to take me to the island of Brač, or at the airport waiting for my grandsons to come from America or for a plane to take me home. But I have other memories of Split,too, in its winter guise, free from the tourist crowds. Years ago, when I spent two winters with my father at the small resort of Primošten, we occasionally came to Split to do some shopping and to enjoy it. My father would sit only in his tweed jacket on the terrace of the Peristyle cafe and read newspapers in the mild winter sunshine of our Dalmatian Coast, while the black granite sphynx, already 1,800 years old when Emperor Diocletian brought it here from Egypt, indiferently looked down on us.

Primošten

As we sped along the Adriatic highway on our way from Split to Šibenik, we passed by Primošten where Father and I had spent three happy winters in the late sixties. At the time it was only a quiet, sleepy fishing village, but subsequently it turned into a fashionable seaside resort. Its name Primošten

Primošten

or " connected by bridge" explains that this was originally a small island, with a bridge to the mainland that eventually permanently linked it with it. When the Adriatic highway was built after the war, Primošten found itself almost over night in the midst of the 20th century. Since then, the tourist industry brought money and profoundly changed the traditional ways of life of this formerly small and modest place. Our visits to Primošten coincided with that transitional period, so we could see how the old gave way to the new. The younger generation readily accepted the innovations that the steady flow of tourist money brought in its wake, while the older generation clung to the ways of life sanctioned by tradition. Old women still wore their traditional black costumes. Some could be seen spinning wool on wooden distaffs while tending small flocks of sheep grazing sparse grass. I have seen them spread their "lancuni", bedsheets, on the pebbles of the beach, securing them with a few stones from being blown away, and leaving the wind and the sun do the rest - dry and bleach them to a beautiful white. Many of them already had washing machines, but they remained true to this traditional way of drying their laundry. And they rode astraddle on a donkey to their small plots scattered over the hills around the village, where they grew tomatoes and other vegetables.

In October people from Primošten gather grapes from their vineyards on the hillsides above the village. Long before the grape gathering began barrels of all kinds and sizes were pushed out to the beach to be cleaned for the new wine. They were washed with the sea water and then left out to dry. Then they were pushed back to the "konobas", a storage area on the ground floor of the house where peasants kept their supply of wine, olive oil, smoked hams, and various tools.

Donkeys were the traditional and convenient way of transporting the grapes from the vineyards down to the village. As in Homer's time, these sturdy and patient creatures would safely carry goatskins loaded with grapes, carefully picking their way along the rocky and often steep pathways. The grapes were then thrown into shallow barrels for crushing. Father and I have actually seen how young boys, stripped to their underwear, split the grape skins with their bare feet. A peculiar smell of fermentation began to drift all over the village and with it the spirits of the people rose noticeably higher. The door of the "konobas" stood wide open, and remained well lit until late at night so that one could see men crushing the grapes. This ancient manner of preparing wine, known to the Greeks and Odysseus, was still practiced in our time, as was the charming custom of announcing that you had wine to sell in your house by sticking an olive sprig at the door post.

However, the old must give way to the new. Obviously, it is better to use electricity than gas lamps, to earn money from tourists, and to live in modern and more comfortable homes. And yet, one feels that the invasion of modern nomads and the affluence that has come in their wake have been paid for dearly. On a more obvious level we are witnessing the destruction of the natural beauty of our coast. Camping sites are usually situated in, or close to forests, and careless tourists often start fires which cause irreparable damage and losses. Another distressing trend is the incerasing number of private summer houses, "vikendice" that destroy the unique beauty of the scenery and the view. But, there is even more reason for alarm when it comes to the old, traditional values that are no longer appreciated. The younger generation readily took as a model for behavior the ideas prevailing in the so-called permissive societies, introduced through foreign films and TV series. Young people in our country found themselves under constant pressure from two opposing centers - the school and the church. The teacher embodied the new socialist order and materialistic principles and ideals, while the priest stood for the spiritual values embodied in a thousand year old tradition. I could learn something of the veiled but nonetheless relentless struggle over the souls of their young pupils from the teacher in Primošten. He told me how the children were quick to sense the tension and competition that existed between the two opposing camps, and how they used it to their advantage. They would tell the teacher they had been to church for their religious instruction taking it as an excuse to miss or to be late for school. Or they would go to play football or simply play truant and as an excuse tell the party concerned that they had attended the class of the other. However, the influence exerted by the Catholic church was very strong. Catholic priests, said the young teacher, had a very firm grip over their congregation, and they continued to exercise it through the strong influence of old grandmothers. And they were better off than teachers, who were moderately paid. The young teacher from Primošten told me how he always refused to accept a ride offered him by the local priest, who, unlike the teacher, could afford to keep a car.

Most of what I had seen and learnt in Primošten that I treasure and remember with great pleasure would have remained unknown to me if I had come for a short visit only - like the walks in the mild winter sunshine that Father and I took along the deserted coast. Occasionally we would come across fishermen hauling in their nets with fish. We usually ended our walk in the village where Father bought his newspaper, which he then read at his leisure in a sheltered and sunny spot of the "porat", little harbor. On our way to the village we always passed by a small, primitive shrine in the shape of a square column on top of which stood a covered altar protected by a glass screen. Beneath it was a Latin inscription which always intrigued me:

Hoc tibi pro votis Catharina
Iurini reliquit
Virgo Dei Genetrix
Tu miserere pia
Anno Domini MDCCLXX
(This shrine Catharina
dedicates to Iurina
May the Mother of God
Have mercy upon you
Anno Domini 1770)

Who this Catharina was, and who was the Iurina to whom she dedicated this modest, moving shrine, nobody in the village was able to tell me. Her father, her brother, her husband, or her lover ? And for what reason was this shrine built ? In memory of a life lost in a shipwreck, or in the war ? But, it is of no consequence. For misfortue and suffering are the common lot of man from every age.

Trogir, Portal of the Cathedral

Trogir — Tragurion

Meanwhile, we were approaching Trogir, a charming town-museum, one of many such towns on the Adriatic coast with a long-recorded history. In the 3rd century B.C. Greek merchants and sailors had established their colony, Tragurion, there which became an important point for carrying out their commercial activities. In the course of centuries Greeks were succeeded by Romans, then by Byzantines and Venetians, and Austrians, a destiny of many other towns on our coast. Croats had arrived and settled down in the region in the 7th century, and they transformed the old word Tragurium to the Slav form of Trogir.

We had time only for a cursory tour through some of old Trogir's treasures, but with the aim of at least paying a visit to its famous 13th century Romanesque cathedral, dedi-

Trogir, detail of Radovan's carving

cated to St.Lawrence. To our great disappointment we found that ancient monument closed for repair, and all we could see of its splendour was a glimpse of the Radovan portal, a masterpiece of wood carving hidden behind the scaffoldings. By its original and free interpretation of traditional biblical themes, taking nature and the immediate environment for its models and inspiration, the designer of Radovan's portal created the most distinguished piece of Romanesque sculpture on our coast.

Trogir, City Tower and Loggia

I had become acquainted with Trogir during my winter stays at Primošten. To walk through the narrow streets of our Dalmatian towns is to go back into the past, and to feel that past almost alive all around you. While you stop to admire a facade of an old house or palace, or to take a better look at some beautifully carved detail on the stone coat-of-arms above its door, you become aware that these towns have had a long and continuous history. Their great attrac-

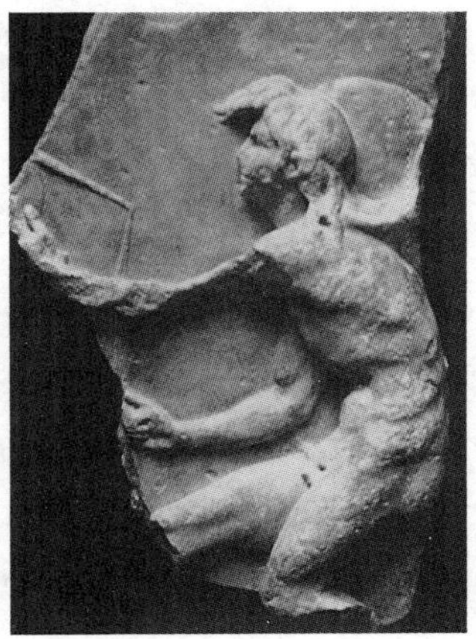

Trogir, Kairos

tion and charm lies in the fact that on the whole they have preserved their traditional urban characteristics, defying the changes of time. Time seems to have stopped in these towns, and as in an open-air museum you can find monuments from different and distant periods - a 13th century Romanesque church next to a Renaissance palace with Venetian windows and balconies, or a building which in the course of time has combined characteristics from different periods.

These stylistic details are of little consequence except for some art historian or a pedantic tourist. For the rest of us there is the pervasive feeling of being in the presence of genuine beauty peculiar to our Dalmatian towns. Ramparts and fortresses, churches and belfries and towers, facades and windows of the palaces, and the palaces and houses themselves, monastery courtyards, city gates and squares, cisterns and fountains - all are made of stone. Everything is made of that noble and enduring material, and it gives those towns an elegant and almost austere character.

The monuments from different periods, the rich Mediterranean vegetation and the pine forests that often come right down the shoreline, the clear and sapphire-blue sea, and the barren and austere mountains that separate and protect them from the harsh climate of the hinterland, all have combined to produce a world of peculiar charm and beauty.

Among the monuments dating from the Greek period especially noteworthy is the fragment of a white marble relief representing Kairos, the god of the opportune moment, kept in the monastery of the Benedictine nuns. Kairos was a god very popular with the ancient Greeks. As in the antique relief from Trogir this god is always represented as a winged youth with wings also attached to his feet, standing on the globe, and with a pair of scales and a razor in his hands. A thick lock of hair hangs on his otherwise bald head to remind you that if you do not seize fortune - the opportune moment - "by the forelock" as it comes your way you have lost it forever. The Trogir relief is damaged, and it is one of many copies and later replicas of the famous Kairos made by the great Greek sculptor Lisipos in the 4th century B.C.

The remains from the Roman times were used as building material, and fragments of Roman monuments can often be detected in the walls of houses in the old part of the town.

One of my visits to Trogir, at the time I was staying at Primošten, is associated with an event I like to remember. It was in January when days are short and when the wind from the Dinaric mountains can make even this part of the Mediterranean cold. As I walked along a quiet and empty street, I was attracted to a hum of voices engaged in a lively conversation coming from behind the windows of an old house I was passing. I could not master my curiosity, and on impulse I decided to open the door leading into the house. When I slowly opened the door it revealed a charming scene. A rather large room was occupied by a group of old people merrily chatting, and leaving a strong impression somehow of community. They all were engaged in different activities. An old man held a skein of wool for an old woman who was busily winding a ball of wool, another woman was knitting, and everybody seemed to be having a very good time, enjoying each other's company. I couldn't remain unnoticed and as I entered the room they made me feel welcome among them. I learned that they were residents of an old people's home. Such institutions are fairly common and have a long tradition in Dalmatia. What made this unplanned encounter particularly memorable for me was the feeling that those

Šibenik, Cathedral (15th century)

old people appeared to be quite comfortable and happy, and in particular the strong impression of warm companionship that they so manifestly shared.

Houses in Dalmatia are built of stone, and except for the "komin", the fireplace, usually in the kitchen, seldom have a stove to keep them warm in winter. To my surprise there was a small cast-iron stove, spreading a comfortable degree of warmth in this large room. On top of the stove stood a large pot full of water. A clever device to save energy and to prolong and preserve the beneficial effect of warmth long after the fire in the stove has gone out - a lesson I have been taught by those old people.

Šibenik, Cathedral, front

Šibenik

We stopped at Šibenik only long enough to pay a brief visit to its famous 15th century cathedral, the most representative example of the Croatian 15th century architecture. It was created by the Croatian architect and sculptor Juraj Dalmatinac, Georgius Dalmaticus (Juraj the Dalmatian), in the florid Gothic style, while final Renaissance touches were added a century later by Nicholas of Florence.

Šibenik, Cathedral, frieze with portrait heads

He has combined the Gothic with the Renaissance into a harmonious whole, and the result is this lovely building of exceptional beauty.

A special feature of the cathedral is its frieze with portrait heads of men, women, and children, sailors and workmen, nuns and other contemporaries of Juraj Dalmatinac, who sculptured their likenesses in stone for the centuries to come.

I wanted my family to see a small church close to the beach, onto which I once stumbled on when visiting Šibenik during my winter stays at Primošten. The church is consacrated to St.Nicholas, the patron of sailors and seamen. I do not know what made me then enter that church, which by its neglected appearance did not promise to hide any great artistic treasures from the past. However, when I entered it I was amazed by the sight that met my eyes. Before me was a whole fleet of model ships of all kinds hanging on iron rods attached to the ceiling. Suspended in the air they appeared to be forever sailing towards their unknown destination. It was on such ships that our brave sailors navigated the seven seas in days past. And these sailing boats, schooners, brigs, and even a steamship with a funnel were votive offerings brought to St.Nicholas by a mother, wife or sister to secure the safe return of somebody dear to them, and to protect the ship and the sailors from shipwrecks, storms and other dangers that threaten the lives of seamen, or as tokens of gratitude for prayers granted.

Šibenik is the only major town on Dalmatian coast that has no classical ancestry. But its steep and winding streets are full of houses and palaces of great beauty displaying styles from different periods. Such walks can be tiring and I have found out that the most confortable place for me to rest is a bench in a church, a trick I frequently resorted to. I have always enjoyed entering Catholic churches in Dalmatia. They are an ideal place for rest with their benches from which you can comfortably contemplate the interior of the church, or meditate. However, there was also always something going on inside the church. Unlike the Orthodox, Catholics are used to frequently visiting their churches at any time of day. I remember listening to a nun playing the harmonium while some old and not so old ladies sat praying in the benches, or simply taking a rest while returning home with their shopping bags from the market.

Once I came upon an old church in a dark side street and on impulse decided to enter it. The church I entered at random looked like many other churches on our coast, but once inside I was quite surprised to see the familiar and traditional symbols of an Orthodox church - the iconostasis and the walls covered with old,tarnished icons, flickering candles and glittering gold halos around the heads of saints and angels. It so happened that it was the day before our Orthodox Christmas, January 6, and the verger and a few old women were busy cleaning and polishing silver and brass candlesticks, and getting everything ready for Christmas Eve. Near the iconostasis I noticed a young monk with a kamilavka on his head and I went to talk to him and inquire about the origin of this church. He told me that originally it had been a Catholic church but it was given to the Orthodox community in Šibenik for the services they had rendered to Napoleon during his brief reign in those parts of our country.

As I was admiring the icons, which were obviously very old and valuable, the monk suggested that I come to visit his monastery, where I could see some really valuable icons, and other treasures kept there. This monastery, Kistanje, is on the river Krka, at some distance from Šibenik, and it would not be possible to reach it except by car. I could, therefore, never have seen that interesting monument from our past if it had not been for a couple from New Zealand, who with their Land Rover were staying at the same hotel with us in Primošten. They were eager to see something that was seldom the lot of common tourists, and the following Sunday we set out in quest of father Vassily and his monastery.

For few days a strong "bura" had been blowing, not the best kind of weather for such an expedition. But we were lucky, for the morning turned out to be calm and sunny, with a beautifully clear sky. Without wind, it was one of those perfect days that you sometimes have in January on the Adriatic Coast.

We started right after breakfast and before Šibenik we turned inland, leaving the good road and the sea behind us, and entered a very barren and austere landscape. It became more picturesque as we approached Drniš, a small town with a medieval castle high on the cliffs overlooking the river Krka, which meandered below it. Before flowing into the Adriatic, near Šibenik, the Krka cuts its way through a deep and narrow limestone canyon of great natural beauty. It forms several waterfalls, the most beautiful being the Skradin waterfall, which consists of a series of cascades, with total height of 48 m.

We stopped briefly to admire the view - a chain of mighty, rocky mountains looming in the misty distance.

From Drniš we proceeded to Knin, another small town with stone houses and a medieval castle. Both towns are associated with the Serb refugees who in 1875 fled Bosnia as the aftermath of the revolt against Turkish oppression. They eventually settled down in their new homeland, and have lived here ever since - one of the many diasporas of the Serbian people.

The landscape we passed through was very pretty in its utter simplicity, small plots of cultivated land with an occasional vineyard and olive grove with bare and gnarled olive trees here and there. All the way we came across flocks of sheep peacefully grazing. Their presence enhanced the rural character of this ancient landscape, where things change slowly and probably look very much the same generation after generation.

When leaving Knin we thought it prudent to ask a policeman for the road to the village of Kistanje, which father Vassily had indicated as a point of orientation on our route to the monastery. We traveled for some time until we began to be beset with some doubts, for we were passing through a sparcely populated part of the country, on a practically deserted country road. When we spotted a house near the road I decided to go to it to ask for directions. The house was simple, it looked almost shabby. I knocked at the door, and to my surprise it was almost immediately opened by a mustached man. I found myself in a modestly furnished room - with a table in the middle and several men sitting and talking around it, among them two small boys, no doubt grandsons of the mustached man. The men were drinking wine, and I noticed a lamb on the spit in one corner of the room ready to be roasted. There was a sense of some festivity pervading the room. The mustached man reassured me that we were on the right road to Kistanje, and as he accompanied me to the door I remarked that they seemed about to celebrate something. He replied, not without a good deal of pride and dignity:

"Yes, tomorrow is St.John, the Baptist, the patron saint of my family, and we are getting ready for the "slava"(a religious holiday observed by Orthodox Serbs). And he pressed me to join them in their celebration and have a drink with them. But I very politely declined his kind invitation, and said that we were in a hurry to reach the monastery. I wanted to leave my somewhat drunk host when he, probably on second thought, made me pause on the threshold of his house, and stretching his right arm towards the distant, barren countryside, said :

"All that you can see around here is populated by Serbs".

And thus we parted. As we travelled along the dusty and empty road I thought that those Serbs must, no doubt, be the descendants of the Bosnian refugees who more than a century ago found security and protection from the Turkish tyranny here, in the very heart of Croatia. However, many

Serbs in this region date back to time of Turkish conquest of the fifteenth century.

The mountains in the distance were covered with snow, and as we travelled on they appeared ever more distant and for that reason even more imposing. We passed through the small and drowsy village of Kistanje, and took a narrow country lane. It was in a sad state of repair with a lot of muddy puddles and pot holes; after a few bumpy kilometres it led us to a broad plateau of peculiar beauty. It appeared completely deserted and the only sign of human existence were two stone buildings, obviously uninhabited, and probably part of what looked like a neglected farm. Two ancient and twisted oak trees close to the bigger building gave it an even more desolate and sad appearance. Sunk in a profound silence, covered only with sparce grass and moss, the landscape was quietly basking in the mild winter sunshine looking mysterious and self-sufficient. Then we suddenly noticed that a young man, standing close to one of the trees, was watching us, I felt almost disappointed to see another human being intruding into this peaceful environment. The boy was glad to have somebody to talk to, and before long we were having a lively conversation during which I learned that he was a student of philosophy at Belgrade University, and that the farm belonged to his parents. He had come home for Christmas and the winter holidays. What a perfect place, I thought, for his metaphyisical preocupations

View of the Monastery of Kistanje on the Krka

and reflections. The magnificent backdrop of the rugged range of the Dinara and Velebit mountains were glittering with ice and snow in the crisp, sunny winter air. As I stood there in quiet admiration I saw on the horizon a series of tiny black dots moving from the distance with great speed in our direction. In no time at all I could distinguish a flock of wild geese flying over our heads on their way to the south. As they flew they broke into several smaller groups that looked like waves making gentle ripples in the air, and then again and again they formed a long triangle. It all happened in a matter of seconds. An accidental witness of this extraordinary scene, I felt privileged to have seen the migration of birds in all their splendour, and I watched them until they swiftly desappeared in the misty distance.

Kistanje

We had our lunch, a couple of sandwiches, sitting in the Land Rover, looking from our elevated position at the monastery of St.Michael, the Archangel, down below on the banks of the Krka River. Its rectangular shape with the church and the belfry looked from the distance like a citadel, but the unique beauty of its position was more reminescent of an enchanted castle. The way leading to the monastery was so steep and winding that one might think only a horse or a donkey, or a man on foot, could reach it, but our landrover safely brought us down to the very entrance gate of the monastery. At first sight the monastery gave the impression of great antiquity, soon confirmed by an inscription in old Church-Slavonic giving the year 1402. We entered through a gate and found ourselves in a stone courtyard with arcades and galleries on all four sides. Their low ceiling was supported with thick, black beams, having several empty swallow nests attached to them. A simple stone fountain stood in the middle, its thin jet of water bringing some animation to this austere environment. Another stone plaque informed us that the monastery was founded in 1345, by Jelena Šubić, the sister of the Serbian Tsar Dušan, the Mighty, and the widow of Mladen Šubić, the lord of Skradin.

I noticed several young men standing idly in the courtyard. I remembered that father Vassily mentioned that the monastery also was a theological school for Orthodox priests in this area. I sent one of those young men to tell father Vassily that he had visitors, and before long the monk came running downstairs, pleased to see us and to show us the monastery. With disapproval I noticed that the place looked neglected, and that it could do with a little more care and order. Everywhere there was evidence of neglect, scattered litter in every corner, scraps of paper, bits of wood, dust, stones, and an occasional chicken and even ox bone were at odds with the dignity and beauty of this place. I found this state of affairs embarassing, and even though the monastery was poor there was no excuse for such disorder.

Before our visit to the Rector we decided to go down to the river. We came across several bee-hives on the sunny side of the fence, and although it was only January the bees were not hibernating. They made a faint, humming noise which made me think of long,drowsy summer afternoons. The river formed a big pond behind the monastery, and it was covered with a thin sheet of ice that in the sunshine looked like sugar icing. Across the pond a long stripe of yellow bullrushes and the coral-red twigs of basket willow behind them made a vivid contrast to the emerald-green water.

Father Vassily took us upstairs to the Rector, who looked very much as an Orthodox priest should. His long, greying hair was tied up in a bun at his neck, and he had a long and thin beard. His pleasant, smiling eyes looked at us through a pair of eyeglasses with a simple, metal rim. The Rector was in the company of another young monk, who was introduced to us as father Jovan. I also noticed that there was another man present in the room. He immediately asked us if we could give him a ride to the village, which we readily promised. The Rector talked mostly about the Divinity School. Thus, we learned that in addition to the theological subjects future priests and monks were taught the subjects that form part of the normal curriculum at our high schools. They also had some Latin and Greek, for three years, and probably learn enough to be able to read and understand some manuscripts. Then, he added that priests were scarce nowadays, and were much in demand. I thought that similar situation obtained in Europe, too, but the Rector added that this deficiency in our country was partly due to the fact that over 1200 Orthodox priests had been killed by the Ustaše during World War II.

Father Jovan, who had left the room for a moment, returned carrying a tray with wine glasses, and we were offered a very good, dry wine, the product of the monastery. It was cooled and very pleasant to drink. When we asked for some more information about the history of the monastery all the Rector was able to tell us was that there are some documents from which it appears that the monastery has been in existence for more than 700 years. The year before, in 1967, they had celebrated its 770th anniversary. Many valuable documents have disappeared in the course of its long history, but the monastery still possessed a large collection of old books and manuscripts in its library.

The monastery had been enlarged several times, and it had been looted by the Turks in 1647. The architecture of the monastery is an example of the late Byzantine-Serbian school.

When we took leave from the Rector, Father Jovan took us to the library to show us some of their treasures. He opened several drawers and took out of them some precious embroideries, miniature carvings in ivory and wood encased in enamel, sacral vessels and crosses made of silver and gold, among them several silver beakers which served as a measure for the wine that was allowed to be drunk by young monks. One of the most impressive things was a book printed in 1459 at Cetinje, Montenegro in the first printing press in this region belonging to George Crnojević. The book is in a perfect condition, and it is kept in a lead box. This book was printed in our country only a little after the first books had been printed by Guttenberg in Germany. We were also shown a Russian New Testament written on fine vellum and beautifully illuminated. Its extraordinary size amazed me, and Father Jovan told us that it was still in use, I could not imagine how they handled a book of such proportions. It looked so big and heavy.

It was sad to see how inadequately these precious books and other sacral object have been protected. On the whole the icons, books and precious embroideries were unprotected from decay and destruction. The ravages of time, the teeth of mice, and mold have badly damaged some of them, including the precious epitrachelion of St.Savo Nemanjić, from the 12th century. On this unique speciman of medieval embroidery 33 figures are depicted with golden thread. The library also harbours a fine collection of old icons, ranging from the 14th to 18th centuries. Father Jovan called our attention to an icon representing St.John the Baptist, adding that this icon was one of their most valuable possessions. It was recently returned to the monastery after it was exhibited in the Yugoslav Academy of Arts and Sciences in Zagreb, which in 1967 had organized an exhibition of the Italian Renaissance painter, Paolo Veneziano. The icon of St.John the Baptist belongs to the school of Veneziano, whose works are scattered in various churches along the Adriatic Coast, and it was painted a little later, in all probability during the 15th century,in Zadar.

At the end we were taken to the church with father Vassily as our guide. I noticed that a religious ceremony was being performed in front of the altar. A man was very piously listening to the priest delivering a prayer, and I at once recognized the man from the Rector's room who had asked us to give him a ride. Father Vassily told me that he had specially come to ask the priest to say this prayer for him, but he did not tell me what had occasioned this particular request. Our visit to the church was brief, for there was nothing much to be seen there. It had no fresco paintings so characteristic of Orthodox churches.

It was getting late and we were anxious to begin our return journey to Primošten. Before we took leave of Father Vassily I asked him what we should do about the man we had promised to give a ride to. Father Vassily told me that the prayer was going to last for some time yet, and that we had better not wait for him. When I was parting with Father Vassily I could not help telling him that he might make his students take better care of this ancient place, which did not deserve to look so sadly neglected. Visibly embarassed, Father Vassily apologized for the litter in the courtyard, and elsewhere, blaming it on the "bura" which had been blowing the previous week. And thus ended our visit to this lovely monastery.

Kornati

On our way to Zadar we passed the uninhabited Kornati archipelago - a group of about a hundred smaller and larger islands which, with their barren and desolate appearance, produce a strange and uncanny effect. But, it was not always so. At one time they were covered with dense woods, but after a fire which raged for 40 days the vegetation, except for lichens and some sparce grass, could not recover.

Kornati Islands

At one point we thought we passed the ill-famed Goli Otok, Naked Island, where Marshal Tito sent those Communists who after 1948 opposed his policy towards Stalin and the Soviet Union.

Zadar

Very tired, we reached Zadar late in the afternoon, and started looking for a hotel to spend the night in. It proved more difficult than we expected. Many hotels had been closed down apparently because of an unusually slack season, resulting from the unsettled political situation and unrest in this part of Yugoslavia; but those which were open were full up.

Zadar, St. Donat (9th century)

Finally, we found a hotel, Kolovari, a substandard one, a little way out from the centre. We decided to take a walk through the town to do some sightseeing before dinner. We knew that this was not the proper way to do justice to the treasures that this museum city could offer, but being short of time we could do nothing better. We soon found that most of the churches we wanted to see were closed down for repair. After this discovery, though betterly disappointed,

Zadar, Benedictine nuns' Convent (11th-12th century)

we felt less guilty for trying "to do" Zadar in such a perfunctory way.

Zadar, too, has a long history. Its natural beauty is manifested in the large number of parks and old pine woods that surround the town and stretch to the very border of the sea. Its past is vividly reflected in the extraordinary wealth of historical and cultural monuments that span a period of more than 2000 years, Illyrian cippuses on the Roman Forum, churches and monasteries, gracious and elegant private palaces display the characteristics of all the major styles, from the Romanesque to the Gothic, Renaissance and Baroque, and tell the strange story of its turbulent past, and of the different peoples who lived along its shores - Illyran tribes, Greeks, Romans, Slavs, Byzantines, Venetians, French, Austrians, Italians. It was known as Iader or Iadera both to the

Zadar, St. Stošija (Eustasia) Cathedral (13th century)

Greeks and Romans. To this day the remains of the Roman Forum grace the center of the town, in the vicinity of St.Donat's church, the latter built by the Slavs in the 9th century with the stones taken from that very Forum. The complicated history of Dalmatia caused Zadar to fall prey to much bigger and stronger neighbors of Croatia, of which it sometimes formed a part. In the Middle Ages Zadar was under Venetian rule and in 1409 it was sold for 100.000 Ducats to Venice by King Ladislav of Naples. It remained under Venice until the 18th century, when it was taken by the Austrians. For a short period it was under French occupation, until 1813, when it was again incorporated into the Habsburg Empire, to be occupied by Italy after the First World War. This occupation lasted until 1944 when, after heavy war devastations, Zadar was finally united with Croatia, and with Yugoslavia.

Romanesque churches of St.Maria (with the Benedictine nuns' monastery), St.Kershovan's church (with its Benedictine monastery), and St.Stošija's - Anastasia's cathedral church, all date from the 12th and 13th centuries. To the same period belong many reliquaries, specimens of the highest quality of the silversmith's craft for which Zadar was famous. Especially fine are those of the busts of various saints, displayed with other treasures in the Benedictine nuns' convent of St.Maria. In the past there had been as many as eighty members in the silversmith guild, but today all you can find are the filigree works of silversmiths who are not native to Zadar. St.Šimun - Simeon's church, with its Baroque facade was actually built in the 15th century and is from the Gothic period. It shelters the silver shrine of St.Šimun, an outstanding example of the work of medieval silversmiths. It was commissioned by Queen Jelisava, wife of the Croatian-Hungarina king Ludovik I (1377-1380) of Anjou, and the daughter of the Bosnian Ban Stjepan Kotromanić. The shrine is decorated with 13 compositions representing scenes from the life of St.Šimun, and bearing Anjou's coat-of-arms. It is guarded by two angels standing at either side of the chest with fully spread wings. They hold the chest so effortlessly that it is obvious that the actual weight of the chest, made of 250 kg of silver, must rest on something else below it. The angels are said to have been cast out of Turkish guns in 1648. The name of the silversmith who made it is also displayed on one of its sides – *hoc opus fecit Franciscus de Mediolano, 1380.*

The Franciscan and Dominican churches were built in Gothic style, and many palaces and houses from the 15th century display a harmonious blend of the Gothic and Renaissance styles. The most notable monument from the Renaissance period is the Town Gate-Porta Terraferma. These are several of the most important monuments, for every street and corner in Zadar speak of its long history.

We did not see much, nor did we have enough time to enjoy and admire what we did see during our brief walk through Zadar. My acquaintance with this town goes back to 1973 when I spent a month in Zadar at which time I got to know the place reasonably well.

I then had plenty of time to spend walking through its streets, admiring old palaces and churches, and I frequently entered them to rest my tired feet and to sort out my thoughts and impressions. It was in the course of one such walk that I came upon the remains of a small church bearing the very strange name of Stomorica. According to local tradition during a plague in the Middle Ages people sought refuge in it, but instead of deliverance hundreds of them were smitten with death. The name Stomorica keeps alive the memory of those people who died in it. On another occasion I came across an abandoned and devastated Renaissance palace, formerly the abode of a noble Italian family, which after World War II had opted for Italy. During the war the Allied Air Forces frequently bombded Zadar when returning from their missions over Germany; even though much of the town suffered from the bombs, it is a miracle that most of the principal churches remained intact. The old part of the town has on the whole been well preserved in spite of the danger that menaced it during the postwar rebuilding period, when enthusiasm so often did more harm than good. A certain number of the old private houses, churches and public buildings have never been restored to their former beauty and glory. Some of those former palaces were occupied by people who had come from all parts of Yugoslavia. They lived in those ruined palaces in spite of the lack of sanitary amenities and water, because they did not have to pay any rent. I once came across a large family of a painter from Bosnia, who made his living by selling his pictures to tourists during the season. They had occupied an old palace with Gothic windows and door lintels, but whose interior was completely gutted by bombs. They had thrown some wooden boards across the hole where once was the floor, using the rest of the house as a convenient dumping ground. In addition to the debris of broken stones and mortar, kitchen refuse and other kinds of trash were taken care of in this manner.

During my wanderings through the streets of Zadar I often remembered Shakespeare's Twelfth Night, which "takes place in a city in Illyria and the sea-coast near it". What place on the Dalmatian coast could the great writer have had on his mind ? Ragusa, or as I would prefer to think, Zadar ? It is not improbable that he knew of these parts if we remember that Ragusan "argosies" went to London, and that Shakespeare mentions "Dalmatians" and "Pannonians" in another of his plays, Cymbeline. Illyria, Dalmatia, and Pannonia were all Roman provinces, and Dalmatia and Pannonia still existed in what until recently was Yugoslavia, while the name of Illyria was used by Romans to refer to Croatia, Dalmatia and Bosnia together.

When Viola, who was stranded on the coast of Illyria, asks the captain of the shipwrecked boat :

> "Know'st thou this country?," he replies :
> "Ay, madam, well; for I was bred and born
> Not three hours' travel from this very place".
>
> (*Twelfth Night,* Act I, Sc. II)

His answer substantiates the supposition that Shakespeare's Illyria could refer to the coast of Dalmatia, whose sons have always had the reputation of being good and brave sailors.

When I now think of Zadar it is not the churches and other monuments for which it is famous that come first to my mind, but rather its parks. Zadar itself and its immediate environment form part of a larger area covered with rich

Mediterranean vegetation. Forests of old pine trees surround the town and reach as far as the seashore. Likewise, whole areas of the town are overgrown with rich greenery. I discovered these parks during my walks through the town. They have been built on some elevated sections of the town, and resting on solid stone walls they made me think of Semiramis' fabulous hanging gardens. Their green areas provided a pleasant and cool shelter, and a harmonious contrast to the ancient stone buildings. At one time they seem to have been lovingly tended, but now they are being left to themselves and their own memories. They have combined their former refinement with the decay and neglect that was slowly but inevitably overcoming them. I often walked along their solitary, shady paths enjoying the atmosphere of profound quiet and seclusion. Everything seemed to speak of things as they had been once upon a time and as they no longer were. The stone steps and balustrades, grottoes with satyrs' heads and hooves, ponds with water lilies and reeds, and other things made in imitation of antique statuary looked somehow forlorn and neglected. While you sauntered among palms, coniferous trees, accacias and mimosas, laurel bushes, myrtles and bougainvillias ablaze with their purple flowers, you almost expected to encounter a dryad pursued by a satyr, or to hear the sound of Pan's reed. Instead, you came across grafitti, deeply scratched into the walls of an artificial grotto - "pederasts, we will not let you have our arses." A crude message perpetrated by some boys, who found it difficult to resist the urge to deface such public places. Occasionally you come across a passer-by who uses these parks as a short cut on his errands from one part of the town to the other - or some exhausted tourists, who seek in them a refuge to rest and to enjoy their meals from paper bags.

Papageno

Do you know how to catch a songbird ? I did not until one day I went for a walk with Mira and Vlatko Jankovic, my friends from Zagreb who taught at the university of Zadar. We walked across an area where pine groves alternated with clearings overgrown with soft, green grass and evergreen bushes. Most of them were covered with berries of different colours, varying from bright red to dark purple. We noticed a large number of butterflies hovering above some large stones. Stones are known to absorb and then emanate the heat these delicate creatures are so fond of. This idyllic picture was somewhat spoiled by the ever-present litter that local people and tourists alike leave behind them. Plastic and paper boxes and cups, nylon bags, and even discarded shoes and slippers, and other human waste were visible in various degrees of decomposition.

As we, with disapproval, commented upon this habit people have, we detected the notes of a song-bird. We looked around and noticed that the singing was coming from two cages placed on a clearing in a pine grove, while two young boys, to whom the birds belonged, were hiding behind some bushes.

"Hello, there", we heard one of them call to us, "Will you, please, move on. Birds may turn up any minute now, and you will scare them away."

The other boy, with a rifle in his hand, got up as if to drive us away. We quickly moved a little farther from the clearing, and I then turned to take a better look of this unusual spectacle. The birds in the cages merrily sang quite unaware that they were being used as a decoy to attract their more fortunate, non-captive mates. They were to be caught on the lime, known as "višć", obtained from mistletoe berries. It was lightly spread over some branches placed in front of the two cages.

My friends told me that this was the traditional way of catching song-birds in these parts, and indeed all over the Mediterranean, and that this ancient art goes as far back as the Middle Ages. It is a good business because song-birds are much in demand. They told me that I could see bird-vendors at the local market.

The market in Zadar is a picturesque place. Peasants from the neighboring villages and from as far as the Vojvodina and Serbia come here to offer their products, eagerly sought after both by local inhabitants and tourists. Home grown vegetables and fruit, grapes and figs picked by hand, cheese made of goat's or sheep's milk, a local speciality, as well as cottage cheese brought from Lika and Croatia are all displayed on numerous stone benches in the market. There is a separate fish market with all kinds of fresh sea fish and other goods that come from our Adriatic. One section was occupied by salesmen who offered things one would never dream of buying but which, nevertheless, miraculously find their customers among tourists. They buy such "souvenirs" as a tangible proof that they had been to some distant and strange place. Leather and wool bags and slippers, carpets small and large, ready-made dresses, hand-embroidered or knitted tablecloths are on sale together with , of all things, home-made African masks, and herons carved of wood, as well as objects made in imitation of genuine folk art, wooden shepherd cups, plates, cigarette cases, and even vases.

One corner of the market was reserved for the vendors of song-birds, where they displayed their little captives in cages of most diverse shapes. These birds always attract a lot of people, both those who come to buy them and those who simply like to stand by and watch the birds and listen to their singing. I often came to the market just because of them. As I watched the birds and their customers I came to learn the names under which these birds are known here. Their names are lovely and sweetsounding like the songs these birds make - vidun, faganelić, gardelin, with yellow and red feathers (goldfinch?), frizelin, which is somewhat bigger than the lugarin and all brown (thrush?), are the most commonly encountered birds on sale at this market.

I once watched a young peasant couple buying some song-birds. The vendor took them out of their cage without much ceremony, grabbing them with his big, clumsy hands, and thrust them into a strong paper bag. The birds were sold at 2000 Dinars each – not a bad business considering that it cost him very little, if anything, to catch them by means of some glue spread on a branch.

I often wondered what makes people buy birds and keep them in a cage. Perhaps they buy them for company. Lonely housewives who stay long hours by themselves at home, and elderly people who have nobody to talk to ? Or do such birds serve to attract customers ? A barber's shop in Šibenik came to my mind that had several cages suspended in his window. They sang so sweetly and looked so charming that Father and I decided he should come for his haircut to that barber's shop rather than to some other.

There is such magic in birds' singing. Their songs have often inspired musicians like Vivaldi and Mozart. Vivaldi has frequently introduced scenes from nature, and his music imitates the singing of birds. In Mozart's Magic Flute Papageno, a birdcatcher, sets his traps to catch birds, blowing on his Panpipe to attract them. And when I hear some airs from the Magic Flute or from Vivaldi's Four Seasons I always think of the sweet sounding voices of our faganelićs and lugarins, birds I first came to know about in Zadar.

Pilgrimage

I happened once to be in the church of St.Stošija at the same time that a couple of elderly American tourists was there, too. They were walking and looking around when they stopped at some stone slabs on the floor, placed on the graves of artisans buried long ago. Each bore a sign of the guild the deceased had belonged to - a pair of scissors for tailors, a pair of compasses for builders. The American tourists seemed to be intrigued by these symbols, and I felt I should act as a self-appointed guide and tell them something about them. They graciously listened to me, and then,I led them to another part of the church to show them an interesting detail bearing witness to some connections that existed between Zadar and pilgrims from distant England - a faded fresco on the wall on the left side of the church, believed to represent Thomas à Becket, the Archbishop of Canterbury. I thought that this little curiosity might be of some interest to them. When I first saw it I had been quite surprised and wondered how his portrait came to be painted in a land so distant from his own. A possible explanation might be found in the fact that the 12th century was the time of great pilgrimages, like the one immortalized by Chaucer in the Canterbury Tales. Canterbury, with the shrine of Thomas à Becket, who was canonized soon after his murder in Canterbury Cathedral, was a well-known meeting place for pilgrims going on their pious journeys. Zadar, too, was one of the points where pilgrims from the north of Europe embarked to cross over to Italy on their pilgrimage to Rome. All during the Middle Ages Zadar was visited by pilgrims coming from all over Europe. Maybe it was at that time that the fresco with Thomas à Becket was painted for the sake of pilgrims coming from England.

During our conversation I learned that the two had come from Italy, and that it was their first visit to Yugoslavia. I asked them what they thought of our socialist country. Their answer surprised me greatly for both of them spontaneously and at the same time replied: "Oh, you are a happy people". For a moment I did not know how to interpret that answer, but they soon provided a comment. What had particularly struck them, they said, was the fact that here they could hear songs coming from all sides.

When we parted and I was out in the street again, still under the impression of their remark, I looked around me with a new awareness. I could hear songs coming from all sorts of places, from a tavern I was passing where a group of friends were sitting at the table, enjoying their "marenda", a traditional midmorning repast, which they accompanied with lovely Dalmatian songs; some people in a boat passing nearby were also singing; and a little farther along, sitting on the steps of the square, two young men with a guitar

Senj, roast lamb lunch out of Senj

were improvising some melodies. A similar scene was repeated no doubt every day, only I had not paid attention to it, because it was so common that I had taken it for granted. I had had to meet those two strangers to make me realize that our people love to sing and do so whenever they can. And this is what happy people do.

That was in 1974, and in 1994 I thought with nostalgia of those peaceful days, when Yugoslavia was still the homeland of all of us.

Senj

We left Zadar early in the morning heading for Senj. The winding Adriatic Highway, which keeps close to the sea, led us through a barren and rocky landscape along the Velebit mountain range.

Senj, classical Senia, is another Dalmatian town with a long and turbulent history. Its fortress, Nehajgrad, built in the 16th century as a protection against the invading Turks, is still well preserved, and its mighty square shape with corner towers dominates the town and indeed the whole nearby area. In its past Senj was an important crossroad between this coastal area and the interior, and has remained one of the shortest ways to Zagreb. We soon turned inland and about 5 km after we had left Senj we stopped for lunch at the Konoba Inn, close to the road, attracted by the delicious smell of lamb being roasted on the spit. While we enjoyed our juicy meal we could hear some guns in the distance, and the young woman who waited upon us, the owner of the Konoba, told us that they were being fired by the rebel Serbian population, disturbing messengers of worse things that were yet to come.

On the last leg of our journey and impatient to reach Zagreb, we rushed over Vratnik pass, and through Brinje, Generalski Stol and Karlovac with its green Kupa River, to reach Zagreb early in the afternoon.

BAROQUE

Zagreb

AFTER THE MEDIEVAL and Byzantine monasteries in Serbia and after the Renaissance towns in Dalmatia, we found ourselves in Baroque and Austro-Hungarian Zagreb. This is the town in which I had passed the most meaningful years of my life. I always return to this town with mixed emotions - with feelings of pleasure to see again the familiar and beloved sights and friends with whom I shared my life, and the feelings of regret and sadness that I no longer belong here.

We had our rooms booked at the Dubrovnik Hotel, conveniently situated in the very heart of the town, just off Jelačić Square, until recently called Republic Square. Our immediate task was to contact those friends who had responded to our written invitations for the cocktail party we planned to give in the hotel in order to assemble and see most of them at the same time. I was a little apprehensive about how my Croat friends would react, remembering a recent snub I received on the phone from a good friend of

Zagreb, National Theatre

mine. When I had heard of some clashes between the Yugoslav Army and the citizens of Zagreb on one of the bridges over the Sava, I called her from Belgrade to find out what was going on and whether they were in any danger. I was startled by her response. She said some very unpleasant things about the Serbs in general, in particular, calling us uncivilized, primitive, and Gypsies, and concluded her monologue by telling me not to call her ever again. I was pleased to see that most of my old friends chose to come, and many asked us to lunch or dinner during our short stay in Zagreb.

My grandson Richard was anxious to go sightseeing and I was very happy to show him some of the places intimately associated with my life in Zagreb. We went first to the Dolac market, in the immediate vicinity of the

Zagreb, the Cathedral and part of Vlaška Street

Dubrovnik, one of the places I frequently visited when I lived here. The sight of the old Cathedral with its two slender neo-Gothic steeples brought back memories of long ago, when we had lived on Vlaška street. The first thing I could see every day from the windows of our flat was the Cathedral and the Baroque Archbishop's palace together with part of its ancient garden, now a public park, a favourite haunt of my daughter as a child. On my way to the Dolac market I often passed through that park, but other times I would go through the old Vlaška street, onetime Vicus Latinorum, with its modest one-story buildings that house artisan shops. Shopping at the Dolac market was always a pleasant occupation for me. I loved to see "kumice", peasant women from the nearby village of Šestine, in their national costumes selling vegetables, fruit, and fresh-smelling molds of butter on large cabbage leaves, brought in large yellow willow baskets. Mushrooms, blueberries and wild strawberries picked on Sljeme, as well as wild cyclamens, and other flowers arranged in small bouquets Biedermeier style, were among the things I always bought together with other edible goods.

Richard greatly enjoyed the bustle and noise of the Dolac market. I took him to the upper part of the market, adjacent to the Opatovina, to show him the statue of Petrica Kerempuh, the Croatian counterpart of the medieval jester and popular vagabond Till Eulenspiegel. This figure from Croatian folklore was immortalized in the Ballads for Petrica Kerempuh, by the Croatian writer Miroslav Krleža.

The Zagreb Funicular

Our visit to Zagreb was too short to allow me time to show Richard even some of my favourite parts of the town. Thus, the Upper Town was left completely out. But while I lived here I had often visited this charming and peaceful oasis of Zagreb which could be reached from different parts of the Lower Town.

In the Middle Ages Grič (the Upper Town today) was surrounded by strong walls provided with several gates which were closed for the night. The bell from the Lotrščak Tower, one of the few remains of the medieval fortifications, sounded a signal to those who were outside the walls, in their gardens, and in their fields and orchards that stood on what is today the centre of the town, to return to their homes. Today, visitors to the town on Grič can enjoy the lovely view of the city stretching below their feet, while farther on across the vast plain they can see the blue Samobor Hills and the far off Klek mountain, believed to have been the traditional meeting-place of witches.

You can reach the Upper Town from several different points. The most common, perhaps, is from Jelačić Square in the centre of the town. You go up the Duga (or Radićeva) Street, which brings you to a couple of steps leading to the old Tower with its Kamenita Vrata (Stone Gate) standing at the entrance to the Upper Town. It is one of the several former gates of the Old Town on the hill of Grič, and the only one to have survived until today. When you enter its low, vaulted passage, at first you are dazzled by the light of numerous candles lit in front of the large altar dedicated to the Virgin Mary, whose icon is protected with a finely wrought-iron screen. The passage under the Tower is black with the soot from the candles that burn there day and night, lit by the people who come to pray to the miracle-working icon of the Virgin Mary. The walls are dotted with small thanks-giving plates offered by those whose prayers have been answered and whose wishes have been granted.

From the same, Duga Ulica (Long Street), a narrow passage to the left leads to Zakmardijeve stube (steps), which bring you to the South Gate of Grič. They were once called the University Steps, because they led to the old University which was at first in the Upper Town.

Another approach to the Upper Town is through Mesnička (Butchers') Street - Vicus Carnificum, a very old street where once stood a city gate separating the town on the Grič hill from the onetime pasture-grounds and corn fields.

Kapucinske Stube (Capuchin Stairways), named after the Capuchin monastery that stood at the top of the stairs, provide the approach from the west. People who later came to live in this house used to speak of strange things - of the organ music and the mutterings of monks' prayers that could be heard there, and of the strange shadows and of the mysterious voices in the corridors of that old building.

There are several other steps leading to the Upper Town, like Mlinarske Stube (Miller's Steps), and Felbinger's Steps, otherwise known as the "Hundred Steps", on the east. But by far the most interesting and attractive way to the Upper Town is by means of the small funicular - Uspinjača - the only public means of transportation connecting the Lower with the Upper Town.

The Funicular is not far from Jelačić or Republic Square, the centre of the town. Only a few steps down the Ilica and the first right hand turn brings you into the short Tomić or Bregovita (Hilly) Street, with the terminal of the Uspinjača. The Funicular with its two blue carriages, each moving every three minutes in opposite directions, has been running since 1889, and is still one of the most popular sights of Zagreb. It has offered its services to tired housewives from the Upper Town who had been shopping at the Dolac market, and whose wellstocked baskets would be too heavy to carry up the steps that wind on both sides of the Uspinjača; to old gentlemen who come with their grandchildren to enjoy the ride in the Uspinjača, watching the two carriages passing each other on their constant way up and down the hill; to the old and the young who either on business or for pleasure go to the Upper Town.

Even though the ride is very short, the Funicular has its rush hours, too, when the offices and schools in the Upper Town open and close their gates. If you are in a hurry and cannot wait for the appointed time for the Funicular to start, it is always ready to oblige you immediately for a small, additional fee. Most of the passengers are its regular customers; they know the ticket-collector and he knows them; they are on friendly terms and exchange greetings, and other polite remarks about the weather and health. Thus, small kindnesses are quite natural here, and sometimes you can have a ride without paying, if you happen to have no small change on you. The ticket-collector knows you and trusts you with the fare until the next time.

The small size of the Funicular restricts the number of passengers who for that very reason seem to be more patient and polite than are the passengers on buses and trams in the town. When the red light gives the signal the door is automatically closed and you slowly begin to glide up towards the Upper Town, covering the distance of 67 metres while you observe an ever wider view of the town that you are leaving below you. At the same time another carriage is coming from the opposite direction, and for a moment the passengers in each can look at one another.

Until 1934 the Funicular was opperated by steam, which was very noisy and smoky. Several people were necessary to keep it going - a fireman (ložač), a mechanic (strojar) and a driver (strojovodja). But, this is no longer the case; everything has been mechanized, and we see and know only the kindly ticket-collector, who is often greeted by some schoolboy: "Good morning, uncle Gašpar, give me a ticket, please".

The Last of the Zagreb Gentlewomen

Many years ago when as a young wife I had come to live in this beautiful town, I got to know a large number of people, many of whom became my friends for life. One of them was Marija S., "the last 'mylady' of Zagreb", as her friends referred to her – half jokingly, half seriously – already at the time of the Second World War when I first met her. But when I became better acquainted with her and her ways of life, I was obliged to agree that this sobriquet suited her quite well.

In spite of the difference in our ages and temperaments I made a lasting friendship with her. There was something in her character and the principles by which she was guided in her life that impressed me at a time when I was still very young and impressionable. I envied the ease with which she moved in life and in society. One of her sayings was that a real lady always knows how to act in every situation. She seemed to know all the rules concerning good manners and strictly adhered to them. She used to say that nowadays very few people had any sense of propriety or of duty to one's own class and social rank. She was a very pious Catholic. For every situation in her life she found an explanation and answer in her deep faith.

Her husband died soon after my friendship with her had begun so that my memories of him remain vague and partial. This is, after all, of little consequence as he does not figure at all in my story. All I remember is that he was small of stature, of excessively good manners, and related to the family of the famous Croatian woman writer, Ivana Brlić-Mažuranić. He was fond of telling stories about her private life, and that is how I learned of the peculiar way she ended her life - by hanging herself in the toilet - a detail not relevant to her beautiful children's stories, but yet, I would have preferred not to have heard it.

Marija lived in the Upper Town, which is built on an elevated area called Grič, and which constitutes the oldest part of Zagreb. This medieval settlement has through long centuries acquired features of different styles, appearing today for the greater part in its Baroque and Classicist guise. The Zagreb Upper Town represents the best preserved monuments of urban architecture in Croatia.

I have always enjoyed my visits with Marija. I liked to pass through the quiet and somewhat mysterious streets of the Upper town, lit by gas lamps, and full of that peculiar atmosphere that emanates from the patina of the old roofs and from its melancholy, neglected gardens. Its streets still preserve the ground-plan dating from the Middle Ages as well as the names of the streets - Opatička, Nuns' street, Kapucinska - Capuchin street, named after the monastery on it, Gospodska - Gentlefolk's street, Mletačka - Venetian street, Jezuitski trg - Jesuit Square, Kamenita vrata- the Stone Gate, and many others. Under their steep roofs each house seems to keep its own secret, unknown to the casual passer-by. The story goes about one house that it is haunted by the ghosts of servants who died a long time ago. They had been poisoned by food prepared in copper vessels, and were hurriedly buried in the cellar of the house. The memory of the Witch from Grič has been preserved and revived in the eponymous and widely popular novel of the Croatian woman writer and journalist Marija Jurić, whose pen-name was Zagorka. The faded stone effigy built in the corner of a house on St.Mark's Square is believed to portray Matija Gubec, the legendary leader of the 16th century peasant revolt. Tradition has it that after they had crushed the revolt, the cruel feudal lords crowned his head with a red-hot iron crown on that square.

The houses of the noble families still stand, but most of them have accommodated themselves to the changing times. The Kulmer palace has been turned into a Gallery of Modern Art, the Baroque palace of the Oršić-Rauch family harbors under its roof the Museum of Croatian History, and the elegant French palace of the countess Buratti, born Vranicani, her former winter residence, has been used for official receptions of the Mayor of Zagreb. Even the house in which Marija lived, in Mletačka street, has its history. At one time it was the home of Ljudevit Vukotinović, a Croatian writer and member of the Illyrian Movement. These facts are commemorated on a plaque displayed above the big, double-door gate. The house was built at the end of the 18th century, and the upper floor was added in the early 20th by the Croatian sculptor Ivan Meštrović. He lived in the house next-door, and the studio in which he worked, together with the house, was subsequently turned into the Meštrović museum and gallery. Some of his sculptures are exhibited in a small garden at the back of the house, surrounded by a wall covered in thick ivy. All of this could be easily seen from the windows of Marija's house.

Thus, every part of the Upper Town tells its story, at every step you stumble upon the past which so tenaciously clings to it. In former days many artisans lived and followed their trade in the Upper Town. Some, like my cabinet-maker, Master Filipović, have remained there until the present day. His workshop was on Opatička - Nuns' Street. A few crooked steps led downstairs into a vaulted area crammed with old and antique furniture in various stages of decomposition or restauration. I often visited Master Filipović when I was in the Upper Town, for I enjoyed talking to him and looking at various kinds of furniture he was bringing back to life. He was a squat, ruddy fellow who instantly made me think of Quince, the carpenter, or rather of Snug. the joiner, in Midsummer-Night's Dream. Master Filipović was just one of the many artisans from Zagreb, a town whose citizens and their well-groomed homes provided enough work for all the cabinet-makers, upholsterers, seamstresses and tailors, to mention but those who first came to my mind. Many of these artisans came themselves to do repairs in your home, or their apprentices came as "moonlighters" to bring back to life a moribund armchair or a Biedermeier sofa with broken springs, or to repolish or patch up a table or a chest-of-drawers.

Marija lived on the upper floor of a house at Mletačka 10. You first passed through a dark vaulted passage paved with big wooden squares, under the inscrutable gaze of two wooden saints, perhaps the guardians of the home, which, at one time had stood on either side on wooden pedestals. They had probably watched visitors come and go from the time the house was built until the day their vigil was brought to a sudden and mysterious end. They disappeared from their pedestals, and Marija thought that they had been appropriated by some "lover of old things". A flight of broad wooden steps would bring you to a glass door provided with white marquisette curtains and an old-fashioned brass knob. You would ring the bell and wait for her maid Marica to answer it. She would open it only a crack to take a cautious look at the visitor before admitting you into a small but very bright entrance-hall. Through its large arched window you could see the Meštrović gallery next door with sculptures in the garden, old roofs of the Upper Town and the medieval bell-tower of St.Mark's church. Marija's flat was a good example of those old-time homes designed not to economize on space but, rather, to provide their inhabitants with all kinds of snug nooks and crannies for various useful and sometimes redundant objects, and which are so sadly missing in modern houses. Marija always received her visitors in the big sitting-room overlooking Demetar Street and the Jelačić palace, now turned into a kindergarten. The shrill and gay voices of the children playing in that garden when the weather was fine, often reached us through the open windows. A mixture of mock-Italian and antique furniture, was arranged with taste in this well-proportioned room. But it was the vaulted ceiling and the parquet floor with polygonal stars made of different kinds of wood that gave the room a special and distinguished character.

It was pleasant to sit with Marija in her beautifully kept room, where everything had its proper place. At one point the door would quietly open to admit Marica carrying a tea tray. In her dark dress and a white starched apron she would noiselessly put the tray on a small serving table with tea cups and other accessories and push it to our table. Then quietly, almost on tiptoes, she would leave the room. Marija poured out the fragrant Lapsang Soochong or Earl Grey tea accompanied always by the same home made savouries and cakes; after a reasonable interval Marica would appear again, and in the same unobtrusive manner take the tea tray away.

Marica had spent 50 years in Marija's household, and she knew exactly when and what to do. After the tea ceremony was over Marija offered us a drink and at the same time thought that it was the right moment to take up her knitting - , or to crochet shawls of the fine, thin wool, she had brought over from France. Her hands were soft and pink, the hands of a woman that had never done any hard housework. All that was performed by her faithful Marica, who had spent with her the greater part of her life. Thus, they grew old together, and Marija kept her even after the war when most households with servants had to do without them. It was considered an oldtime luxury out of place in a socialist state, which actually few people could afford under the new circumstances. Marica had no close relatives and Marija felt it her duty to keep her even when it was not easy for her. In recognition of Marica's good services, Marija had provided for her in her will so that Marica would not be left destitute after Marija's death. However, destiny has decreed otherwise, and Marica died before her mistress.

The shawls produced by Marija were later sold at a milliner's shop, but Marija also made such shawls for her friends if they asked her to do so. Once, I asked her to make such a shawl for me, and was quite appalled when I heard what she charged for it. However, she calmly told me : "I wish I could give it as a present to you, unfortunately, I cannot afford it". I never knew what her situation was like after the death of her husband. But she knew how to make the most of the small pension he had left her by him, and to keep up appearances. Her knitting was one way of supplementing her modest income, and she began giving private lessons, in French, Italian, German, and English, all of which she spoke almost equally well, having learnt them in her childhood. She possessed the shrewd and practical sense of the people coming from the Croatian Littoral, and when the opportunity presented itself she bought the flat she was staying in for a paltry sum of money. Yes, she was really very businesslike, in spite of her often repeated statement that she was impractical and helpless.

On one occasion, when I was drinking tea at Marija's, our conversation took an unexpectedly personal turn. It was not her habit to introduce personal topics into her conversation, and so I was quite surprised to hear her ask me whether I would consider being converted to Catholicism. Her argument was that my husband as well as my daughter were both Catholics, and that it would be quite natural for me to become one,too. And she added that she would be very pleased to act as my godmother. I was stunned by that question and felt very embarrassed, not because I did not know how to answer it, but rather because I did not want to hurt her feelings, and maybe lose her as a friend. To make things worse it happened at the time of the great persecution of Serbs by the Ustaši, which made me, as a Serb, very unhappy. Being married to a Croat I was in no immediate danger, but it made me even more sensitive to the suffering of my less fortunate fellow countrymen. I do not know what motivated Marija's suggestion, but I suspect that she thought that under the circumstances I would be safer as a Catholic. I told Marija that my religion was chosen for me by my father, and for that reason I would always honour it. She accepted my refusal with a good grace, and we remained good friends ever after.

After having spent more than 20 years in Zagreb, I moved to Belgrade where I began a new life. I missed Zagreb and my friends there, and once a year I went on "a pilgrimage" to Zagreb, mostly to visit my old friends. I always visited Marija, of course, but on one such visit I was greatly surprised to hear that she had moved to live in a retirement home. It was so unlike her, so contrary to the brave and courageous way with which she managed her life. To me it appeared a surrender. However, when I went to see her there, she told me that she had decided to give up her flat at Mletačka, after the death of her old Marica. Her whole life depended on Marica, for while she was alive she looked after Marija's well-groomed flat, and cooked and did other things for her, leaving Marija free to give private lessons, and in general lead the kind of life she had always been used to. Without Marica, all this fell to pieces; the change was too much for her, and so she went to live in one of the Zagreb homes for retired people. But I shall always think of her as "the last of the Zagreb gentlewomen".

Cocktails

The cocktail party we gave at the hotel was quite well attended, and I think that it was a success in spite of the fact that several of our close friends and even relatives either could not or possibly did not want to come. But those who did come gave us much pleasure, and in their friendly and warm company we spent a couple of happy hours. Their presence more than compensated for the absence of the others.

It is interesting that nobody attempted to discuss the political situation, which was, no doubt, very much in the mind of all present. The only unpleasant memory in this respect is related to a school friend of my daughter's, who came to visit us one afternoon at the hotel. The conversation revolved around the split between the Serbs and Croats, and our young visitor put all the blame on the side of Serbs. She did not hesitate to qualify them as an uncivilized people, who had brought Croats nothing but primitivism and the "boot", the expression used in our language to denote brutal and rough force. I was quite startled to hear her speak thus, and could not refrain from reminding her that she was too young to remember when Croatian Ustaše persecuted and butchered the unprotected and innocent Serbian population in Croatia during World War Two, something that could not be qualified as civilized. In spite of that I never attributed this barbaric behavior to all Croats. It was sad to see that young people, like this friend of my daughter's, could be so ignorant and intolerant.

We saw Richard off for America. At the airport I noticed an unusual amount of activity going on; passengers were examined much more rigorously than usual and asked a lot of questions before being admitted to the check-in counter.

On our way to Belgrade we practically had the whole of the Brotherhood and Unity Highway to ourselves. There was hardly a car to be seen for hours on end - an unusual and disturbing sign, for this is the main and only road linking the western part of Yugoslavia with the east, and connecting Zagreb to Belgrade. In retrospect I have come to see this paucity of traffic as the first clear sign of Croatia breaking away from Yugoslavia.

We reached Belgrade early in the afternoon, and after a brief rest at my sister's house, Paul and Rina continued their journey on to Hungary. I stayed with my sister, who had not been able to go with us on our Yugoslav tour because of her chronic problems with asthma.

We parted very pleased with our tour, and full of shared memories and impressions. Little did we suspect then that it was the last time we were to travel through what was known as Yugoslavia.

BROKEN CONNECTIONS

Letters from Zagreb 1991-2

November, 1991

Dear Borka,

————————,I am sending this letter with the diplomatic bag to make sure you will receive it. We know that you, poor things, get there only counterfeited news. Here, it is terrible.

– M.M.Croat

December 6, 1991

Dearest Borka,

————————, no one can advise you, and I do not presume to do so, but may it not be true that in fact a return to Zagreb would be least lonely to you ? I simply do not know how your very Croatian friends may be reacting at the moment, so what I say may be wrong, but basically I think many of them are true friends and if you have inherited your sister's flat you might be in a position to do a good exchange since I am told that there are many people trying to go from Zagreb to Belgrade and fewer the other way. But, as I say, I may be a bad adviser here for I cannot feel as a Croat (though since Vukovar and Dubrovnik and now the villages all round Osijek I feel more Croatian than I ever did before - and I identify myself with those poor battered people as I never did - for battered and bulldozed they are to an extent that you in Belgrade may not be aware of - but which was made explicit in the letter to all the world press signed by 30 Nobel prize winners to say that the conscience of Europe could no longer stand by looking at the wanton and brutal destruction being wrought by JNA - and still more explicit in the report sent by the Europen Commission to the Hague 2 days ago in which it spoke of a cowardly army targetting hospitals and schools and churches in towns and villages indiscriminately and themselves keeping outside. It is an evil thing that is being done and I am sure that many Serbs must themselves be shocked and must be aware through foreign radio in spite of your heavily censored press).

– B.B. English

February 16, 1992

Dear Borka,

——————, this war is tragic for all of us, but it is perhaps particularly terrible for you, as you are in more than one sense torn between and frustrated by your feelings and attitudes. I am sure that you disapprove of the official policy, of the war and the killing - in fact I am convinced that you dissociate yourself from all kinds of violence, and yet, I think that some things that exist between Croats and Serbs (there are things between heaven and earth, my Horatio) were brought by this war to the point when they had to end in a disagreement. Disagreement, of course, is no reason for friendships to cease, but it is sad that a man belongs to a civilization in which it is inevitable. On another plane, however, to belong to a different nation poses today very real and cruel obstacles to our freedom of movement, drives people into extreme situations, and often isolates you in your own environment.

– S.S. Croat

February 22, 1992

Dear Borka,

——————. In your letter you have mentioned the extreme reaction of one of your "oldest" friends in Zagreb. You did not mention her name but I know well who you were talking about. She has been verging on extremism for a long time and even before the fighting began had become very much so. However, I believe that many people in Zagreb have had their tolerance shaken by some things that have happened, and so I believe that it would be difficult for you to go back even if you should wish to do so.

– B.B.English

May, 1992

Dear Borka,

—————, a few months ago I wrote a circular "political"letter for my friends, but I do not think it appropriate to send it to Belgrade. I shall send it, perhaps, to your daughter in USA. We had better not talk politics again, but nowadays a man appears to be a hypocrite if he pretends that the problems that determine the course of our life are of no consequence. You and I, however, have been friends for such a long time that politics cannot substantially affect our relationship.

– S.S.Croat

May, 1992

Dear Borka,

—————, I am happy to hear that you will go to America to join your children there, for it will never again be pleasant to live here, in the Balkans. I wish you all the best, and do not forget us here, where in times past we were so happy.

– P.P.Croat

May, 1992

Dear Borka,

______________. I see that you have gone to America to be close to your only child. Much as it is hard for me to think that you have gone so far from us, we who have loved you so dearly, nevertheless I think that you have done well and done it at the last moment. Zagreb is no longer what it used to be. Serbs are disparaged and abused everywhere, and are intensely hated. However, I cannot say that for my Croatian friends. All but one are extremely good to me, and their friendly feelings towards me have been not in the least changed.

– G.G.Serb in Zagreb

September, 1992

Dear Borka

______________, we are all well considering our age, and we hope that so are you, but what we are going through is really terrible. This is the third time we are experiencing a war, and this one is the worst of all. What the Serbs are doing could not have been conceived even by the most fiendish brains; they have brought us, Croats, to the brink of material ruin, and they have wiped out the Bosnian people. All these refugees are an unbearable burden for us...

– D.D.Croat

September, 1992

Dear Borka,

——————, first the widow of my mother's brother came from Osijek and stayed with us for about 3 months, then in April my cousin from Sarajevo came with her little daughter and they also stayed with us for 3 months. Fortunately, I was able to find them a flat " to be taken care of" in the absence of the owners, which is only until January 1993. What will happen then, I have no idea. My other cousin and his wife have stayed in Sarajevo -without electricity or water- but with shellings and bombs instead. They had the opportunity to come to Zagreb, too, but the moment they leave their home somebody else will move into it, or first rob it and then settle down in it. It is not easy to give up everything without any hope of a more stable life, without a pension, without money.

– M.M. Jew

September 26, 1992

My dear Borka,

I was surprised and not surprised to get your letter from the USA. Not surprised because I knew you were going, and surprised because I did not know that you had already gone.

I can hardly imagine the turmoil and emotions you must have experienced in your last months in Belgrade and your deep sorrow that so much fighting is now going on where you and Branka lived as children. I am afraid the old Tuzla that I remember reading about several winters ago, in the pleasant surrounding of the Kristal Hotel, where you later came and had tea with Emilio and me, does not exist anywhere now except in your memories.

I do not know how many accounts of present-day Zagreb have been elicited by your letters. What is certainly true is that however difficult things are in Croatia, and they are difficult in all kinds of ways, they are better than they were a year ago. A year ago I had just left Ljubljana airdrome for Heathrow, with my two grandchildren, with the fear that something like what is happening to Sarajevo might happen to Zagreb. My son and his family lived in what was then the war zone, though only 25 km from Zagreb in the front line and from the opposite bank of which there was for 8 months constant mortar attack on the people and villages of Pokupsko. Nothing happened to them though things dropped in several places not far away, but the villages and especially the churches (particularly favoured objects of target practice or slivovic shooting soldiers) not far away were badly damaged although not so badly as many villages in Eastern Slavonia or in Krajina (all those lovely Slunj wooden watermills burnt, parts of Plitvice centuriesold forests cut down, whole villages erased). My son himself was in the Croatian army for 7 months, he narrowly missed being sent to a very bad part of the front because the army needed someone to translate a manual and someone else thought of him. Many of the people in his company were later killed.

That is now already past as far as Croatia is concerned, though not as far as those people from the occupied parts are. There people still cannot go home to their villages (some of them where their families have lived for generations, and most of them in villages well over 50%) for fear of "cleansing". I made a slight break in writing this letter to look at the news and one of the items was still Croatian and Hungarian families being driven out of Baranja (driven out by threats of bombs, threats too often carried out to be ignored, or of personal reprisals against some family member, usually a son or husband).

All this, of course, pales when one knows what is going on in Bosnia – and nobody able to do a thing about it but look on. We must not fight because we are supposed to have signed a cease fire, the UN troops cannot because that would go beyond their mandate – they are allowed only to look on at what is happening.

That is the background against which we all live and know that for us at least it is better than when I took off one year ago. Just to walk the streets of Zagreb you would not know there was a war going on except for the number of young men in uniform and occasional young wounded walking across the square. Our main everyday problem is poverty of just the same kind as after the last war. No one can meet their expenses from their income or pension, and there are few extra jobs for most people to do. Numbers of people are now having their electricity or phones cut off because they cannot pay, and few people have anything to heat their homes with or cook with wood nowadays so when winter comes..... Luckily for me and for my children the translation field is holding up.

– B.B.English

Letters from Belgrade, 1992.

September 10, 1992

My dear Borka,

Thank you for the telephone call and the letter. ——
———.

I know that you are interested in what things look like here. Always the same, but a little more difficult for the very fact that they have been lasting longer. Everybody is dreading winter, and the lack of fuel. And because of the shortage of heating oil, the consumption of electricity for heating will probably result in the "break-down" of the system. How beautiful.

The influx of refugees from Bosnia has again become more intense these last few days. After the London Conference Karadžić ordered the Serbian Army to withdraw from Goražde. After their departure the other side began with systematic killing, persecution and torturing of Serbs in Goražde itself and the surrounding villages. Those who could, have left. I obtained this piece of information from a French woman journalist. I cannot remember if you were still here when a newspaperman from the London Independent announced that the UN has been informed that the civilians waiting in a queue for bread (in Sarajevo when 16 of them lost their lives) were not killed by Serbs but by Moslems. However, the damage had already been done. Nobody paid any attention to this piece of information. A few days ago I was listening to some French Blue berets (on the radio) who said that they are tired of keeping silent, and that they can no longer hide the fact that they are being killed by Moslems, and for this reason becoming an easy target for them. Even some French officials admitted that 2 days ago 2 of their soldiers had been killed by Moslems, etc.

My son is waging a battle, from morning till evening, with the SPS (Socialist Party of Serbia) over the electoral system. The Opposition is for a proportional and the Government for a majority system. The Federal government has organized a Round Table on the electoral system, financing all the parties as well as the TV and the press during the pre-electoral campaign. However, there is little certainty that the Government will give in. If not, the Opposition, at least its greater and more important part, will not vote. Then, again we shall have elections that nobody but the Government will recognize.

– V.V. Serb

September, 1992

Dear Borka,

——————, my brother and his wife extricated themselves from that hell at the very last moment. It is now a month that Sarajevo has been without water or electricity, while the fighting is going on unabated. According to our information the truth about us hardly gets through to the outer world, but in spite of the established facts many still refuse to acknowledge them.

And what should I say about the Slovenes and their conduct ? My brother was obliged to sit at his daughter's house while she was trying to get from the police a piece of paper that he is temporarily living with her as her guest, and that she will guarantee for him morally and materially during his stay in Ljubljana. He is being treated as any other foreigner without documents. At the moment he has gone to Trieste to visit with his daughters-in-law there. The Italians honored his old Yugoslav passport but the Slovenes refused to admit him with it. We are daily in touch with him by phone, the Slovenes, however, apply strict sanctions (against Serbs), and have cut all connections between us (Serbia and Slovenia).

– Dj.Dj.Serb

November, 1992

Dear Borka,

I know that you are anxious to learn what is going on here. During the last few days my friend received 2 letters from Sarajevo, through the Red Cross. Her grand-daughter says that she does not want to lie to her, and that it is terrible there. For the last 3 months they had water and electricity only for a couple of days. They eat mostly rice and sit in cold rooms because all the windows have been broken, and there is no fuel nor will there be any for the coming winter. The letter was written a month ago.

Here, in Belgrade, everything is pretty much the same, only more so. Federal,republic and local elections are being organized, but the conditions are impossible. The Opposition and the authorities are conferring, but with extreme difficulties. The authorities, of course, do not really want an agreement, and the days for the election campaign are already running out. The election day should be on December 20. There is ,however, still hope that the elections will take place. Of course, everything would be much better if the Opposition were really united, and if some individuals for their personal ambitions, jealousies and other fine qualities did not upset the united activity of the Opposition. However, Depos (Democratic Movement of Serbia) still exists.

Everyday life is the same as it was when you were here, only more difficult. The prices are rising and so does crime. Refugees keep arriving. For days on end negotiations have been in progress with the Moslem authorities to let the women and children, the sick and the old leave Sarajevo. However, things are moving with great difficulty. Convoys for Split are going, but not for Belgrade. In the last few days, however, some 400 people have been allowed to go (out of Sarajevo). A crowd of several thousand people have been waiting for 3 days standing at the Sarajevo railway station for a permit to leave. At night the temperatures drop to 5 below zero. Allegedly, they will set out on foot for Pale. Nobody knows what is going to happen.

– V.V.Serb

November, 1992

My dear Borka,

——————. What should I write to you about us and our situation? Everything is as it was while you were here, only it is worse in every respect. Let me begin with Bosnia. The belligerent parties have become exhausted for neither side has large reserves or resources, and all but the Moslems have attained their ends. The Moslems are the principal losers in this war. They have been left without the land, without a number of smaller and bigger towns, and the population is for the greater part gone into exile. My relatives on my father's side – from the neighbourhood of Modriča,

Gradačac and Doboj – are all in exile. Some are in Koprivnica, some in Germany, some in Hungary or Pula, Zagreb, and some are here (in Belgrade). This is not to say that the Serbs have fared better. However, at least they have the "satisfaction" that "they have won" militarily. But we know what kind of victory this is – dead people everywhere, others in exile, territories cleansed by either one or the other side, with the worldwide reputation of opprobrium we shall not be able to acquit ourselves of for the next 50 years. And yet, our politicians refuse to come to their senses, each person harping his own strings, and fighting each other. Sarajevo has become a veritable Dante's Inferno – people leaving daily, and it is doubtful whether anybody will remain there. I have talked to some who had arrived here – they burn parquets (floor for fuel), there is no regular cooking any more, they eat corn or semolina flour dissolved in water, they have all lost 15-20 kg, alternately there is no electricity or water, everything is sold and bought on the black market for D Marks only. Those who have some reserves manage somehow, others are condemned to starvation and death. The other day I received a long letter from Tuzla through the Red Cross from our friend M.Z. The situation there is terrible, but still a little better than in Sarajevo, there are no snipers there, so they can go to Simin Han and Bukinje. otherwise they are in a blockade, food is rationed. The town authorities did not allow segregation on a national basis, therefore there are no incidents, retributions etc. in that town.

But, there are some 50.000 refugees, they are in a very bad state because no help from the Red Cross or UNPROFOR can reach them as the passage over Majevica is controlled by Serbs, and to go via Kladanj is very difficult. Thus, while they themselves are starving they must also provide for a large number of refugees who have flooded the town and settled down in the flats of those people who have gone into exile. Our Tuzla seems to be the only town in all of the former Yugoslavia which is still existing in some sort of togetherness, but for how long, remains to be seen.

– M.M. Moslem-Serb

Buttikon, Switzerland, September, 1993

Dear Borka,

————————, my wife and I are now here in the village of Buttikon, near the little town Wollen, staying with my daughter and her husband. Until two months ago we were able to telephone our neighbours in Zenica but since then all communications have been cut. Some people dressed in uniforms have taken a TV set and a video from our flat, having first broken two locks in the door, under the pretext of making sure there were no snipers hiding there. The flat remained open for a couple of days, then an honest neighbour, a Croat by nationality, repaired the locks and has looked after the flat as far as it was possible. The flat is now occupied by my daughter's friend and her husband and their small child. They had come as Moslem refugees from Foča without anything of their own. We shall send our consent from here so that they can remain in our flat and in this manner prevent its being requisitioned, for there are over 20,000 refugees at present in Zenica.

– J.J.Serb

Belgrade, Decembar 14, 1992

Dear Borka,

————————, I understand that you have had some bad experience with the Polish authorities during your journey to the USA. Visas seem to cause ever greater difficulties wherever you go, and one needs a good deal of energy and patience to face the endless waiting in order to obtain a visa for European countries. That is why I probably won't go to the Tyrol any more, and I was so much looking forward to it. My son tells me that in Vienna our people have to wait for 3 days and more, from the break of day, in order to obtain a visa for our country.

Here, everything is very much as before, only refugees are arriving at a faster pace as the fighting in Bosnia continues, and famine is rampant. With the winter coming it is estimated that the number of victims of hunger and cold will reach 150,000, but I believe that to be exaggerated for from Serbia alone help is coming in a steady flow.

We are all in great expectations because of the elections, which will take place on December 20. If the Opposition wins, which is far from certain, things will get better in every respect; if, however, it does not happen nothing good can turn out for us either in this country or abroad.

– R.R.Serb

Letters from Zagreb, 1993

January 15, 1993

Dear Borka,

——————, if I had to characterize the most important things in my life in the last two years, I would say that the saddest is the war against Croatia, which has left us devastated and has ruined the chances for a better life to my generation. ——————.

For month on end I have been sitting glued to the TV set or with my nose stuck into the newspapers, or else dissipating my energies on endless and ennervating and exhausting political discussions, and foreseeing and anticipating events. For months we have not been to the theatre or cinema not because they did not exist but because I did not feel like going there, or because it seemed to be a sin to have a good time. Our social life with friends was also stagnating, nor did we go on holidays. While the world abroad was gradually assuming the shape of a chimera, for we have become paupers for them. ————.

As a complement to this letter I have enclosed the letter I wrote yesterday in English for my colleagues abroad – for I am aware that you and I are lagging behind as far as current information is concerned. I shall not edit it for you, as there is nothing offensive in it, however, some psssages would have been phrased more delicately if I had written it to you. In our further correspondence we need not insist upon it at all, but until now we haven't exchanged our views since the war began, so I think that I must once tell you how I view this highly tragic moment of our history. ————

——.

I wish you to settle down well in your new homeland: "Don't turn aside and brood on life's bitter mysteries".

– S.S. Croat

February 16, 1992

The war has not disrupted my family or destroyed my property, but it has been a terrible upheaval in our life. First the news and images of destruction, and the fleeing masses of people (with bundles, and small children on their arms, in tractors, on bicycles, in army trucks). Then the same masses of people (about half a million) scattered all over the remaining parts of Croatia, creating great economic and psychological problems, some living in hotels on the Adriatic, some in gym halls, sleeping on pallets. Then the massacre of soldiers but also of many helpless civilians: horrible, medieval, inhuman. Hundreds of thousands of innocent civilians have been driven away by threats and brutality, and their houses razed to the ground : the usual scenario is shelling or dynamiting, followed by sacking, burning down, and sometimes a final levelling of the foundations with tanks. Then the cattle is either driven away or left to die without food or water (I heard on the radio the other day that 124.000 heads of cattle have perished or been lost in this way).

My reaction to this has been a complex mixture of despair and hatred, not only of the "enemies" who until recently were my compatriots, but also paradoxically of my own country and of myself, a revulsion against the realization that one has spent one's whole life in a country where such things are still possible, where civilized life is in constant jeopardy. Besides, we (the Croats) are not quite blameless either : there has been much rashness, strident slogans, diplomatic mistakes, political intolerance, all the way from the beginning. Also, our ruling party leaves much to be desired, and the general level of our political and democratic consciousness also leaves much to be desired.

The problem as I see it is an infernaly complex mixture of historical circumstances which have thrown all the nations of Yugoslavia as if in a conjuror's hat and yet - as they were made of hard stuff - never let them merge. The Croats and Serbs have remained Croats and Serbs, with a vengence, (this is a historical fact and none has the right to expect them to become Yugoslavs if they won't), but many Croats and Serbs have also become Bosnians (and many of them are now Moslems by nationality). The national diversity was first exacerbated by the autocratic Serbian monarchy between the wars (which supressed Albanians and Croats), then by the Nazi conquest during WW II, and finally by Communist rule (its political supression of healthy national feelings and its supression of normal economic development, both of which created endless frustration). In the course of history our mutual borders have been endlessly redesigned by Turkish invasions and the conquest of other great powers, and the concomitant endless migrations, mostly of Serbs, and in recent times the expansion of Albanians. It is all I repeat, infernally complicated. And yet, in spite of its murky depths (perhaps unique in western civilization) the current state of the problem is as clear as day. While, after the fall of communism, Croatia and Slovenia had democratic elections and a national reawakening which was anti-Yugoslav, Serbia retained a communist regime which found a natural ally in the communist Yugoslav Army : their two strongest ties are rule by force and a pro-Yugoslav stand. Everyone today knows something of our recent history. What is important to stress, however, is that all the disputes including the central one I have just outlined could (should) have been solved by political means, not by force. Here comes what is as simple as day : although the Serbs had a case, not a hair had fallen from any Serb's head in Croatia after the elections, and they could have brought their problems (e.g. the political autonomy for the Knin region) to Croatian and international diplomatic tables. Instead, the Serbs began an armed insurgence in Croatia, and this insurgence was supported by the Yugo-Army and soon transformed into an incredibly brutal war of aggression on Croatia by a vastly superior military force. Thus, although this war is deeply rooted in ethnic (and other problems) it is not an ethnic war. It is a war of aggression – all of it is conducted on the territory of Croatia – and with the exception of the Knin region, on the territory which apart from a number of villages does not have a Serbian minority.

The US are implicated in all this by the fact that for many good reasons (and as many bad ones) the US were strongly committed to keeping Yugoslavia together. They also had some good and also some less good reasons to dislike some aspects of the new Croatian regime. Besides, they knew we were small and needed their help, and in short, they stalled while we were being butchered (and, alas, as time passed sometimes also butchered in return), in unspeakable ways and on a scale absolutely unpermissible at this time and place (in the middle of Europe, at the threshold of the 21st century). Luckily the Germans and some other Europeans finally also decided that this must be stopped, and paradoxically and ironically it was the Germans who saved what remained. If the Germans had acted only a week later, what remains of Croatia would also have been heavily damaged: the large cities Rijeka, Split, Zagreb and their great shipyards and industries.

After the latest cease-fire the prospects seem brighter. Still, I foresee an endless haggling about when and where the blue helmets should be stationed, a protracted and potentially dangerous crisis in Bosnia, especially as America wants a total solution of the Yugoslav problem, where Serbia always gets precedence as a potentially strong Balkan ally (most of Croatia is not Balkanic to begin with but rather Mediterranean, Central European, Danubian/Pannonian). It will also be infinitely difficult to get the Army and Serbian irregulars to vacate the territory they have occupied (now 26% of the entire territory of Croatia). Besides, the damage of this war – the deaths and maiming, the loss of property, and above all the hatred is immense, and for decades to come irreparable.

There can be no doubt that in spite of many initial errors Croatia is the tragic victim of a barbaric war caused by a combination of communist terror and the Serbian myth of dominance in this part of the world. And this war has caused infinite, apocalyptic destruction.

On another, less apocaliptic level this war has wrought havoc in the lives of liberal intellectuals of a western orientation such as myself. Hard-working, civilized and decent, we have spent our entire life in the shadow of war, financial crisis and political repression. And thanks to this war, this will also in some measure be true for the foreseeable future. For many years to come our values will not be the priorities of this society which will needs be dominated by warriors, militants and crude primal nationalists. I see a new primitivism rearing its head and the thought that it is finally a new Croatia and in the long run democratic primitivism is not of much help at this moment. Of course, the change from communism to our present system is something no one can underestimate. It has been a truly great step from a communist dictatorship in the direction of a democratic society. But I have become impatient with all primitivism. I crave for some, even the most modest, cultural and civilizational luxuries that my colleagues in the west can take for granted. Some of these could be bought with money which has suddenly become so extremely short. Others are more delicate flowers, which have literally been nipped in the bud by the war. We think it is to us, the specialized gardeners of more tender plants, that this time and place have been and are particularly unkind. But then one remembers those whose houses have been levelled with tanks and who have lost their sons, whose parents had their throats cut on the doorsteps of their cottages, and one is back in the world of apocalypse, violence and guilt from which one has been trying to escape all one's life....

And so it goes, in endless, maddening, frustrating circles which seem to take us further and further away from European standards. But, Europeans beware ! In spite of much sympathy and kindness in some quarters there has also been enormous lack of understanding in others (French intellectuals, British and American ruling structures). In spite of appearances, deep down (as the Texan says in Catch-22) we are regular guys like you. This war is your misfortune as well, you are responsible for it just as we are, even more perhaps, because we are all products of European history, and that history was made by you, our Big Brothers, more than by us. And if we go down, tied to you by thousands of invisible threads, we shall drag you down with us, down down, corrupting your high standards, disrupting your social order, haunting your dreams.

– S.S. Croat

January 3, 1993
Dear Borka,

——————, the reason I have not written was that I did not know what to write to you. I have been in a state of a total shock and stress caused by the acts of savagery, cruelty and barbarism, of killing and massacring, raping of women from 16-60 years of age, of destruction of houses and properties, churches and towns, graveyards, kindergardens, hospitals, of devastation of material, cultural and spiritual goods and treasures of Croatia. All these horrors have been conceived by the Serbian Četniks and the Army under the command of Serbian generals. This was and still is an agressive and genocidal war waged by Serbs against all the others and in particular against Croats and Moslems. It is not an ethnic or civil war as it has until recently been qualified by the west and the USA. It is ethnic cleansing and persecuting of 2,000,000 people; refugees, banished from their looted homes which subsequently were settled in by Serbs on occupied Croatian territory. Today we are left without 30% of our country, lands which have been historically inhabited by Croats.

If it were not for the charitable individuals and organizations and our emigration abroad, we would all have starved and frozen to death, as they still are doing in Sarajevo. Some people are still in concentration camps, or have dissapeared without a trace.

After I somewhat calmed down and after the situation in Croatia was a little improved over the 70% of the territory I tried to think rationally. All this was strange to me for I have never chosen my friends on a national or religious basis. To understand it a little better I have read the history of the Serbs from 1389 until today and have learnt some incontestable facts. Let me begin from the beginning.

It is indisputable that the war was waged on the territory of Croatia, historically established land, with a Croat majority population.

The aggressors for the most part are Šešelj's Četniks supported by the Army under the command of the Serbian generals.

Thus, Croats have not attacked Serbia but defended themselves as best as they knew how and could, for in the first phase of the war we had neither any army nor any arms.

The instigators of this terrible tragedy are the intellectuals who drew up the Memorandum in the Serbian Academy of Arts and Science with Dobrica Ćosić as their head.

The intellectual and material concept is the idea of a Greater Serbia, a morbid conception that has existed for many decades, a claim that all Serbs must live in one state governed by Serbs. For the 20th century it is a paradox that cannot be understood in a civilized country.

The Serbian Academy has transferred the execution of the plan to Milošević who, together with Šešelj and some others, must carry it out. The Croats, however, realizing what was at stake fought back with tenacity to defend their country; many lost their lives or remained maimed bravely fighting against the stronger Yugoslav Army and the Četnik aggressors. An incredible moral strength is awakened in you when somebody attacks you and wants to take everything away from you.

I am struck by the fact that both the intellectuals in the Memorandum and common, uneducated people are under the same obsessive idea of a Greater Serbia; an incomprehensible idea for the end of the 20th century.

I was even more impressed by the fact that the Orthodox Church until very recently has stood by Milošević and his methods of conquering somebody else's territory.

This brings in the crucial question about the origin of such actions by Serbs.

It is certain that revenge for 1941 was at the bottom of this idea.

Mass media- TV and the press have inflamed imagination with the idea that all Croats are Ustaši, which is a notorious lie because I lived in the period of 1941-45; however, it is a subject apart, and about its veracity I would not like to argue.

In my opinion the material basis and other privileges enjoyed by Serbs in Croatia were not proportional to the number of Serbian population; access to recreation centres and resorts, cars, high positions in the army and the police, high salaries etc. Belgrade has centralized huge funds of Yugoslavia, including those from Croatia.

In conclusion, what I have just described does not apply to Serb democrats, to the Serbs who have publicly disassociated themselves from these horrors, like for instance Ljuba Tadić (which I have included in the letter), and above all it does not apply to the Orthodox Serbs in Zagreb, who together with us are experiencing the same traumas. For the time being, however, the elections in Serbia have proved the fact that the majority of Serbs have voted for Milošević and his policy.

Let me tell you at the end that Serbia and its people are obsessed by the idea of their original identity, for me it means an underdeveloped consciousness of oneself; such an idea would never occur to an Englishman, a Frenchman or German at the very end of the 20th century.

As far as I am concerned, we, inhabitants of Zagreb have no such worries, we can go to Mirogoj and read the names on the tomb monuments and know who we are and where we have come from.

Ivo and I have been lucky to have been spared such horrors, our children are close to us, well and alive, and well provided for, so that our family has fared well until now. You have the good fortune to be near your family, in peace and prosperity. May you continue to be so happy.

– Greetings from L.L. Croat

February, 1993

Dear Borka,

————————. Do you know what we here constantly wish for ? Peace, peace, then good health, and then peace again, and then all over again, because without it there is no real happiness nor contentment.

We hardly ever go out now, we do not feel like it any more, most of the time we watch TV program – but more often than not we do not feel capable of watching the horrors of destruction and devastation. Sarajevo has just been shown – it is short of not existing any more – everything burnt down, distroyed, looted. My cousin and his wife finally left Sarajevo in the last convoy – for months they had lived under shelling. Each took only a small suitcase only – and said good-bye to everything they have had. Their journey to Split lasted about 30 hours (in 7 buses with 700 people, among them 80 Jews, about 100 each Serbs, Croats and Moslems- organized by the Jewish Community from Sarajevo). The old and the sick were later sent on to Makarska – nobody knows for how long. It was moving to hear them on the phone, they told me that after 8 months it was a bliss to be able to go to bed satiated and lie in peace. The other day I cried while watching children's ward in a hospital in Sarajevo – children with amputated arms and legs.

————————. In spite of everything women in Zagreb are elegant and well-groomed, you do not feel that Croatia has to support 750,000 refugees (500,000 out of them mostly from Bosnia).

– M.M. Jew

March 22, 1993

Dear Borka,

————————. Sarajevo is practically burned down, the trees in the parks cut for burning. It is a little better in Tuzla, however, they have several thousands of refugees - and they themselves have not enough to eat for the town is blocked up. The situation in Eastern Bosnia is terrible (Goražde, Srebrenica, etc). People daily die in their tents of hunger, illness while many freeze to death while fleeing. In Croatia there are 600,000 refugees from Bosnia alone, and there many more from Vukovar, Glina, Petrinja and Ilok, where everything had been distroyed and burnt down. As a result we have a high inflation and a rapid fall in the standard of living of the middle class. However, we in Zagreb are lucky because we have water, electricity, gas and petrol, and you can buy everything if you have money, if you cannot get it here you can easily go to Austria or Hungary.

– M.M. Jew

Letters from Belgrade, 1993

Belgrade, 29 Janvier, 1993

Ma chère Borka,

——————. Je sais, bien sûr, que Votre pensée vient souvent par ici et que Vous devez être malheureuse du spectacle desolant qu'on y voit.

Mes amis Yougoslaves sont profondément déprimés, et, pour beaucoup la vie devient difficile... et je sais que, comme étrangère, je ne vois qu'une partie de la réalité. Ils ne se plaignent pas mais leur détresse est évidente.

Par les liaisons que Vous avez ici Vous en savez sûrement plus que moi. ——————.

Mon mari a beaucoup de travail... les diplomates font beaucoup d'efforts pour essayer d'aranger les mécanisms diaboliques mis en place... vraiment on ne pourra pas leur reprocher d'avoir laissé faire... (ce que l'on entend souvent!) Mais sans doute ont-ils mis du temps à comprendre (si cela est possible) la complexité des multiples problemes. ——————

– B.B. Française

My dear Borka,

——————. I am sure that your thoughts often come this way, and that you must be unhappy because of the sad sights you can see here.

My Yugoslav friends are deeply depressed, and for many of them life has become difficult...I know that being a stranger I can see only one side of the reality. They do not complain but their plight is very much evident. Through your connections here you learn more about it all than I do.

My husband has much to do...the diplomats put a lot of effort into trying to bring order to the infernal mechanism put into motion...indeed, they could not be reproached for having let things go their way (which is so often done !) However, it took them a long time to understand (if this is possible) all the complexity of a large number of problems.

——————.

– B.B. French

December 23, 1993

My dear Borka,

——————. Here it is so terrible that I had better not write about it.

——————, all this together with incredibly high costs of living have forced us to celebrate our patron saint's day (St. Nicholas) in the narrow family circle. To tell the truth nobody feels like having guests or preparing for such celebrations any more. ——————.

– K.K.Serb

September 20, 1993

Dear Borka,

——————. I must first appologize for not having written to you for such a long time. In the first place this terrible situation here, high cost of living, poverty, and then we had a move which occupied me for quite a while. My daughter, her husband and her daughter are now living with me. We think that it is better to be together amidst all this calamity in which we live. I admit that there is more work now, but on the other hand I am no longer alone. It is true that for many years I had lived alone and now I must get used to living in a close company.

Here, things are going from bad to worse, you would be surprised at the change since you left. Everything is terribly expensive, and anyway there is hardly anything to be had. I now regret I did not buy some canned food a year ago when it was still available for there are none any more now.

– K.K. Serb

December 10, 1993

My dear Borka,

—————, here there is nothing specially new, except that every day things are getting worse and worse. An egg today is 100 million Dinars, and my last pension cheque was 500 million, so you can imagine what it is like. We are facing a complete economic and financial collapse, only God would be able to pull us out of it. In the midst of this madhouse we are having election on December 19th with tens of different parties which are basically all nationalistic – they all want Bosnia to be partioned and the Greater Serbia. Even if by some miracle the war came to an end we would still have to face taking stock and paying the debts. Tuzla has held out long enough, however, the extreme elements there seem to have arrested the legal town authorities, and who knows how it will all turn out.

You have left at the right moment and managed to organize everything well, which you would not be able to do today.

– M.M. Moslem-Serb

March 25, 1993

Dear Borka,

—————. No doubt you are informed about what is going on here through the TV and the daily press, even though it is for the greater part onesided – just about the same as we are here presented with the news from the point of view of one side only. As a result the majority of people have become indoctrinated in one way or another. Nobody, dear Borka, knows what to expect. The American aviation will only increase the general confusion reigning here. The suffering of the people in Bosnia is enormous, and nobody actually knows the true extent of this catastrophe. In any case more people have been so far killed than in the so-called Desert Storm in Iraq. Here (in Belgrade) where there is no war, inflation has played havoc; my pension has been reduced to 32 DM, and will continue to go down, while prices are going upward and are changed every Monday.

I am in touch with Sarajevo, sending parcels to a cousin and some friends there through the Adventist Church and their relief organization ADRE. They are very reliable and deliver parcels to your door. One of my relatives died in exile while another was killed by a shell in her flat. My father's village, Tarevci, has been completely evacuated and has gone into exile in Croatia, which is the worst option as they are not welcome there and are given no health protection, their children cannot enroll in school,etc.

– M.M. Moslem-Serb

March 28, 1993

My dear Borka,

——————, our nerves are completely ruined, there is no end to our "agony". Everything has already become hard to obtain while the prices are astronomical. The so-called democratic world in the west seems to be set to completely ruin our people. Worst of all are human victims that are falling every day, not to mention the devastation of the country. There are now over 600.000 refugees in Serbia. They must be fed and provided for. But, enough about this tragedy of ours, which seems to have no end.

– Dj.Dj. Serb

April 8, 1993

Dear Borka,

——————, we are more or less well, however, the prices are going up every day in huge leaps. Our salaries and pensions are increased, too, but they are lagging far behind the prices. Medicines are beginning to be in a short supply and so are many other things. However, we manage somehow to bear up, though with much difficulty. The number of refugees is growing, from your Tuzla alone 18,000 Serbs wish to emigrate, but the Moslems won't let them go, both in Tuzla and in Sarajevo. Our factories have almost stopped their production, as a result crime is on the increase. Worst of all is the lack of fuel so that a large number of trains and city buses do not function. However, God will take care so it all turns out well, as our people say, in spite of the fact that our dear God has become senile and no longer knows what he is doing.

Here, we live in a kind of fever on account of the situation. This morning we heard that the Assembly of the Republic of Serbia in Bosnia has turned down the Vance-Owen plan, and decided to solve the problem by a referendum. And the imbecile that is leading the USA can hardly wait to apply force against us, but luckily for us, except Germany, he has no other followers in Europe for such a proposal. Unfortunately, he can carry this on his own, and if that happens, it will be merry, and we in Serbia may also get our heads knocked.

– R.R.Serb

September 15, 1993

Dear Borka,

————————, since September we have been given ration cards for basic food articles - flour,oil, sugar, salt, detergent, etc. So, we have returned to where we were in 1945. Food stores are practically empty, but at the open air market you can buy vegetables and fruit, at excessively high prices. Even worse than the shortage of food is the shortage of money, both in banks and at the post-offices, so that people wait in long queues for a couple of days before they can get their pensions. Both the Government and the Opposition have manifested their complete inefficiency both in politics and economy. Nor is there any other political body that could promise something better, such as trade unions, youth organizations,etc. All those who are responsible as well as individuals seem to have been paralyzed, as if drugged, and are powerless in every respect. Powerful mass media, especially the TV, have done their work well, they have leveled the consciousness of the people and made them incapable of thinking independently, let alone do the critical thinking. Each clings to "his" nation and to "his" TV, and thus they go on harping what the politicians have dished out to them, and the latter are without precedent in history. Indeed, it would be hard to make any comment about them, for you do not know which of them is more stupid, narcissoid and power-loving. They have ruined the people, scattered them all over the world, and imprisoned them in towns under blockades, and now they are playing the part of peacemakers.

I can't tell you much about my relatives and friends in Tuzla, but I do know that there are no persecutions or reprisals there, only a huge number of refugees and no provision. As far as I have heard people manage to survive - but how, they alone know. Zenica is in a much more difficult position, and Sarajevo is the worst off of all, and so is Mostar now, too. The two most beautiful cities in the country have been destroyed so thoroughly that not even Hitler's "stukas" could have done it better. People who write from Sarajevo say that they have lost up to 20 kg or more, and that they are without water, electricity or gas. Their life is as it was in the Stone Age. At the market goods are bartered for goods, or gold and jewelry.

Dear Borka, you left at the right moment – but I know that you think of us and that you often wish you were here. Over there, they harp on the same string : Serbs are the only culprits for this war, which is nonsense. The dishonorable side of this whole scenario is their ignorance, ineptness and the overbearing behavior of the super-powers in their quest for self-fulfillment at the expense of a small country. However, their propaganda apart, we should actually blame ourselves for what has happened to us. When I say "we" I think of the leading politicians who proved to be unable and unprepared to safeguard their own country only because of their megalomania and grand nationalistic plans, including the war...We shall dearly pay for their craze and madness, because people have been en masse entangled and involved in mutual retributions and crime,in plunder, etc. For those of us who have no "our side" in this war it is very hard, especially because of the bleak prospects that await us...

– M.M. Moslem-Serb

November, 30, 1993

My dear Borka,

I know that you cannot stop wondering what is the matter that I haven't written to you for such a long time. There is nothing the matter except our great depression and absence of strength and will to do anything else except to maintain the elementary functions of life going. ——— ————.

The circumstances in which we live, to put it mildly, are terrible. We are exposed to an unprecedented genocide in every sense of the word. The so-called "civilized and democratic west" is applying such measures of terror that we may disappear even if it was not from the immediate consequences of the war.

Life here is in general very difficult, the rate of inflation is terrifying. Prices change several times a day so that many articles are ten times more expensive from one day to the next. On top of all that cold weather has set in rather early this year. The sanctions have made the import of goods and fuel impossible so that cold weather will finish us off. The supply of electricity is still good, but we are threatened with restrictions. There is no gas or other solid fuels, nor spare parts for the repair of power plants.

I am sorry that I have nothing better to tell you, my dear Borka, but I am so oppressed by our harsh reality that

I am mentally quite exhausted. The more so because our generation had its youth ruined by World War Two, and our old age is ruined now by the misfortune that has befallen us…

– Dj.Dj. Serb

December 13, 1993

Dear Borka,

————————, your letter travelled one month, but the main thing is that it has arrived. I am not surprised at all, because a lot of mail does not reach us any more. My son communicates with my brother in London by fax. We do not have one but my brother sends it to a school friends of my son's. ————————.

I have heard from some people that D. is now living together with her daughter and her family. They have done what many other families have already done, to gather together to live at one place so that they could let out one flat in order to increase their income. Flats are let for D Marks only.

From here, I have nothing good or nice to report. The situation is getting progressively more difficult, while it is impossible to catch sight of the end of the war. A few days ago an economist said that our inflation is in forth place in the world's all-time list. Hungary was at the head of the list immediately after the war, but it lasted very briefly, then came Greece in the mid-fifties, also not for long, and Germany at the beginning of the twenties. However, we may already be outdoing Germany...

Our pensions amount to no more than 10 DM. I think there is no way for your pension to be sent to you in USA, it would all be spent on postage and bank expenses...

– V.V. Serb

Buttikon, December 14, 1993

Dear Borka,

______________, the news from Bosnia is so bad and disturbing that I no longer want to listen to the news or to watch the TV. In the last year and a half about 400,000 people - women and children - have been killed in mutual quarrels. We still dare not to return to Zenica.

______________. We have heard on the Belgrade and Sarajevo TV that several shells had fallen in the centre of Zenica, and killed over 15 people. So far, Zenica and Tuzla have been the most peaceful towns. Zenica, I hear, is full of refugees from eastern Bosnia, and we have also heard that some Croats and Serbs have moved out of Zenica, that there are a great many "mujaheddins" from Pakistan, Iraq and from other Islamic countries, who have joined the Bosnian army as volunteers...

– J.J.Serb

Belgrade, October 22,1993

Dear Borka,

——————. Our situation is terrible, both from the economic and political points of view. If my sister did not send us Dollars from America, we would already be living like true paupers, as do all those in Belgrade who have no relatives out of the country, or some reserves "hidden in the mattress" (in the bank, as you know, it is no use having foreign currency), or like black marketeers and war profiteers, or members of the ruling class. A new class, new bourgeoisie, is emerging from those profiteers, you can see it with your naked eye. If, by some miracle, you were here, you would be very much surprised. All our supermarkets are completely empty, one empty section follows another. Both milk and bread have recently become very scarce. And what is available comes in insufficient quantities, besides you never know when they will appear in the shops. People spend two hours or more waiting for milk, and even then, you can seldom get 2 lt; sometimes you get nothing. That is how long you must be prepared to wait, if you want to have milk every day. In addition to that, transportation has become one of the worst problems. You can see fewer and fewer buses and trolleybuses in our streets; there is no gas, no spare parts to be had.

I know that you are curious to hear what my son is doing. I connot remember if you were still here when

DEPOS (the Democratic Movement of Serbia) was formed. At the time he was very active, but he left them before the elections in December, because he was in favour of boycotting them. Now he is again head over heels in politics. The pre-election madhouse is about to begin again. Milošević has dissolved the Parliament and has set the election for 19 December, following the 10-day discussion about confidence in the Government. The question of confidence was posed by Šešelj, after the Radicals and the SPS (Socialist Party of Serbia) had parted. As usual, there was no unity. From the first I was of the opinion that this situation should be taken advantage of to overthrow the SPS if possible. The leaders of the opposition are divided. One part thinks as I do, the others maintain that they should not vote, not even against the SPS, since that is what šešelj has advised. As you see, an even more interesting period of two months is ahead of us.

– V.V. Serb

Letters, 1994

Belgrade, January 12,1994

Dear Borka,

I see that you are worried because of our situation and because of the bad reputation that we have acquired. We have become immune to it, and have become accustomed to it, but the news that reaches us from Bosnia is truly terrible. The other day a lawyer from Tuzla came to my office, and we talked of many things. He told me that relations among the people are bad, but not too bad, however the leading group of people bears a considerable blame in spreading the intolerance. ——————.

I asked him why he had left Tuzla; he said that the scarcity of food and of other necessities, like electricity, water, and fuel caused him to leave Tuzla. Moslems, however, do not allow you to leave the town, so that he was obliged to escape over the mountain with the help of the local peasants, and so got himself out of a tight situation. This, Borka, is a small picture illustrating the circumstances prevailing in Bosnia.

Here, in Belgrade, charitable societies constantly distribute food (in parcels) free of charge in the streets and on the squares, and the queues are sometimes longer than a 100 m. The independant TV station often broadcasts the comments that are heard by the people waiting in such queues, and often you can hear how they curse and blame Milošević who had brought it all on them, but he, of course, cares little about it.

They have now promised to take economic measures to liquidate the inflation, they talk other nonsense,too, as if we were such simpletons as to believe them.

When medicines could be obtained I was obliged to listen to my friends talking about the kinds of pills they were taking, about their blood-pressure, etc., now at least I am free from such stories because medicines can no longer be obtained in pharmacies.

– R.R. Serb

Maribor, January 10, 1994

Dear Borka,

——————, accept our belated but sincere wishes for the New Year,1994. May our hopes come true that peaceful times without terror and suffering will come back again. With all our heart we wish that you may be able to revisit your homeland and all the other parts of it so dear to us all. We spent the summer in Volosko, a great many changes have taken place there; no foreign visitors any more; and the local people keep to themselves - they listen to the news and stare at TV. No songs can be heard, unemployment is rampant while the prices are getting higher and higher, in spite of the fact that shops are well supplied. The Belvedere Hotel, Blue Grotto and Ivka , as well as other restaurants are all open. The marinas in Opatija and Ičići are packed with beautiful motor boats and yachts. There are still people with a lot of money. So much about our seaside.

Here, in Slovenia everything is quiet; we still live quite well.

– T.T. Slovene

Buttikon, November 10, 1994

Dear Borka,

————————, nothing very much is happening here, days go by and we continue to live at the expense of our daughter and her husband. It is out of question for us to think of returning to Zenica. Zenica is a Moslem canton (enclave). People of the Serb nationality have gradually left Zenica except for a few rare individuals who have remained there at their own risk. The report goes that there are Mujaheddins as well as Moslem extremists in Zenica, they have also their military base there, and the centre for religious education. Here (in Switzerland) we often listen to the radio news both in Serbian and Croatian, Radio Belgrade and the Voice of America, as well as some broadcasts in German and the BBC from London. Disorder in Bosnia has become so widespread with the assistance of foreign countries and Islamic states that it is impossible to prognosticate the end of the war.

Hundreds of thousands of people have been killed and the country has been terribly devastated, half the population of Bosnia and Herzegovina live as refugees all over Europe. Some have been summoned to return to their villages and places twice, and twice in six months they became refugees again, thanking God that they have remained alive.

The Croats are tense also, for they do not agree in everything with the Moslems…

– J.J. Serb

Belgrade, December 1994

Dear Borka,

————————. We are well acquainted with the situation and the frame of mind of the people in the USA, but are unable to understand why a country with such vast possibilities is uncapble of having for two terms in succession an able president, nor why it cannot choose its representatives, senators and congressmen, who would be equal to their role. My son, Vojo, has an interesting comment, he says that this incapacity displayed by Americans is a sign of their great strength, for if America were not so powerful, it would not be able to put up so often with various incompetent and ignorant persons.

Here, always the same situation, incessant shooting and killing, as if human lives were toys. The other day I watched Moslem prisoners-of-war from the front around Bihać – all of them kids 19 years old. Our authorities there let them go wherever they chose to go but many of them decided to remain there for good. All that Izetbegović had to say to that was that Moslem women would quickly make up for the loss. A nice comment!

Serbian and Croatian politicians are true brothers, even though Croats disown us: both are real thickheads, so much so that even American congressmen cannot compete with them. Serbian Assembly is so pittiful that you cannot imagine it. The ruling party does what pleases it, the opposition is completely disunited and mutually hostile to each other, as if they were the worst enemies. Only the Serbian Presidency at Pale is equal to the situation. They are serious and they know what they want, and what cannot be agreed upon. However, they are under an awful pressure on the part of

Milošević, who views them as his enemies that should be liquidated. Nobody knows what it will all come to. Croats, too are very much divided, and do stupid things galore, much to my surprise, because I had thought them to be more intelligent. At this moment Tudjman has nothing more important to do than to "cleanse" Croatian language of "Serbisms". For example, you must not say/write "kolovoz", because it is Serbian, but you must write "kolovlak" instead, you must not say "naročito"(for the same reason), but "osobito", etc. *ad infinitum,* as if he had no other more important business to attend to. Slovenes got freightened by Italians, and quarrel with each other about Istria, which Italians keep an eye on, and which can easily devolve upon them.

– R.R. Serb

EPITAPHS

Revisiting the Former Yugoslavia, 1994

In May 1994 my daughter Katarina and I went on a brief visit to what until recently was still known as Yugoslavia. She wanted to attend the 35th anniversary of her graduation from the Classical Gymnasium in Zagreb, and that was a good opportunity for both of us to revisit our former homeland and see old friends and what family we still had there.

The preparation for the journey was long and elaborate, both of us needed visas for the parts of the country that had become separate since we had last been there in 1991. My daughter who, unlike me, had an American passport also wanted to renew her old Yugoslav passport, with which she had originally come to America in 1961, and which she had kept renewed. The new Yugoslav Embassy in Washington D.C. however delayed her application for weeks, and finally refused to issue her the passport because her birthplace was in Bosnia and prior to immigration to the USA she resided in Croatia. I, on the other hand, was obliged to seek the intervention of a senator to speed up my Croatian visa. As we planned to visit both Belgrade and Zagreb, which were now separated and had no air or land connections as before, we were obliged to choose Budapest as a connecting point from which we traveled first to Zagreb. In order to go to Belgrade we had to return to Budapest and thence by a private bus to Belgrade. And then again to Budapest in order to return to the States. All this contributed to a considerable waste of time, and money, of course, but on the other hand it gave us a chance to see many things which would not have been possible otherwise.

Budapest

When we left our plane in Budapest we were almost immediately assailed by several people who were offering private transportation to Belgrade. Belgrade was cut off from the rest of the world because of the embargo imposed by the West in protest of Serbia's support for the Bosnian Serbs. There were no international flights or train connections, but the resourceful Serbs found ways to cope with the adverse circumstances. So, I was not in the least surprised to be surrounded by a group of young people offering to transport us in comfort and safety to Belgrade. We took a card with an address and telephone number from a very young, energetic, and good-looking girl, and told her that we would give them a ring to fix the time when we returned from Zagreb. Then we drove off to our hotel - the Astoria - in the center of the town, which was known to my daughter from a previous visit to attend a scientific meeting. I also had memories of Budapest when my sister and I had stayed in Zakopane in Poland in the winter of 1974, and had spent a day sightseeing in Budapest. The city is conveniently situated half way between Belgrade and Zagreb, both of which have had long associations with it.

A ride through Budapest in late afternoon left me with the impression that this old city on the Danube looked somewhat dirty and sleepy. Ponderous buildings dating from the 19th century looked gloomy. The Astoria Hotel still retained its oldtime charm, reminescent of the Napoleonic era and imperial decorations associated with it. Only male waiters served you in the dining-hall, in the middle of which stood a large and lovely vase, Sevres perhaps, exhibited on a pedestal and protected by a glass cover, with scenes from Napoleon's campain in Russia and his retreat in 1812. A small orchestra played discreet Hungarian and Central European tunes during our evening meals. These tunes were soothing and sweet to my ears, recalling past, happier times. It was a pleasure to be there.

The following day we took walk through the streets in the vicinity of our hotel. On a little square close to it some elderly men discreetly standing by the walls of the houses were timidly offering passers-by small bouquets of flowers or home-grown vegetables. They did not look like professional vendors but people who in that way sought to earn a little extra money. There was also an old woman quietly begging. Only a few steps farther, in front of a church, a healthy young woman who might have been a peasant, was offering some handiwork, embroidered tablecloths, napkins, and doiles, to some tourists who did not want to buy. She was so desperately soliciting and pleading that my daughter ended up buying a tablecloth for $20 from her. These people were signs of the economic crisis Hungary was going through. The experiment with democracy and western style capitalist free market economy did not show encouraging results in Hungary. I remember having read somewhere that because of the economic difficulties and the growing unemployment the formerly defeated Communist party was again gaining strength in Hungary.

My daughter spent the greater part of the morning in the Yugoslav Embassy trying in vain to arrange her visa for Belgrade. People coming from different parts of the world who needed either an entry or transit visa were silently and moodily waiting in a long queue. Some apparently had waited for several days without succeeding in obtaining their visas, among them a peasant couple from somewhere in the Vojvodina who had lost, or had had all their money and other possessions stolen in Budapest. They were waiting for help from the Embassy, and told my daughter that they had spent the night in the street. These scenes were indicative of great changes that had recently taken place in these parts.

Zagreb, View from Railway Station

Zagreb

We went to Zagreb by train, following the same route that had existed since Austro-Hungarian times, when Croatia was still part of the Habsburg Empire. On the train we shared the compartment with a young Russian lady and her son, who were traveling from St.Petersburg to Kraljevica in Dalmatia, where her husband was working at the shipyard as an insurance agent for Russian ships. The conversation was very interesting, for Tanya Konstantinovna was very willing to talk about the life in Russia today, and the difficulties resulting from the dissolution of the Soviet Union, and their struggle to establish a western capitalist style of economy. From her it became evident that most people think that the old communist system had many advantages in that there was no unemployment, and health services were accessible to everybody free of charge. She also told us that she found life in Croatia, especially food, very expensive.

It was strange to travel to Zagreb with a passport. I stepped onto the platform of the well-known Zagreb "kolodvor", railway station, with mixed feelings of pleasure and anguish. Once again as we left the railway station I was looking at the familiar panorama of Zagreb as it presented itself to me – the King Tomislav statue and the fin de siecle Pavillion of Modern Art behind it, the crowns of the old plane-trees on Zrinjevac a little farther away, and in the distance the silhouette of the neo-Gothic cathedral, clearly outlined against the dark-green range of the Zagrebačka Gora. Hundreds of memories surged up from the past to claim my attention. In Zagreb, for many years we had lived in the close vicinity of the Cathedral, and I went to Sljeme for long walks, together with thousands of other people from Zagreb, almost every Sunday. But, there was no time for reminiscing, we needed Croatian money for a taxi to take us to the hotel. At a small exchange office at the station the clerk told us that they were just about to introduce the new monetary unit, the "kuna", which was in circulation during World War Two, and had therefore desagreable associations, for some people at least.

We would much sooner have walked along Zrinjevac to our hotel, *The Dubrovnik,* which was only a short distance from the station, but our luggage made it necessary for us to take a taxi. The driver, who easily recognized us as visitors from abroad, took full advantage of our ignorance of prices and the value of the money. He charged us several times the rate, which in American money amounted to something like $12. We realized we had been had after it was too late.

At the Dubrovnik Hotel, where we had a room reserved, we found only one message waiting for us at the reception desk – from a schoolfriend of mine from Tuzla, wishing us a welcome and inviting us to dinner. I was disappointed that other friends of mine from Zagreb did not respond to my cards from America in which I had announced when we were coming to Zagreb. We decided to call some of them just the same. And as my daughter justly supposed it turned out that several of them meant to leave a message, but for one reason or another had not done so. In no time we had so many invitations that we could not manage all of them.

Zagreb, Tkalčićeva Street

Dolac - Tkalčićeva

The brevity of our visit dictated which of our favorite haunts we could visit. The obvious and the nearest choice was the Dolac market, practically across from our hotel. The market with the stalls and the "kumice", peasant women from Šestine, and the statue of Petrica Kerempuh looked very much the same - a welcome illusion of permanency. We descended the steep and short Skalinska Street and found ourselves in my beloved Tkalčićeva Street. This is the street on which my late friend pek Vdović, the baker, and his first wife who was so fond of extravagant hats, used to live. His house was close to the corner of Skalinska Street and I had no difficulty in identifying it. But, my friend, the "pek" was dead long ago, and with sadness I remembered that it was he and his wife who had bought my neo-baroque bedroom

Zagreb, Opatovina

furniture, and thereafter we had been friends. I took pleasure in telling my daughter that when she was already in America pek Vdović and his wife had invited me once to a Sunday lunch, and on that occasion I for the first time had heard of the "Sunday beggar", an institution apparently peculiar to Zagreb. During the lunch, which we had had in their small, dark kitchen, some strange music coming from the verandah aroused my curiosity. Pek Vdović explained that it was their "Sunday beggar" playing his zither. I had never before heard of such a thing and I was eager to learn more about it. Pek Vdović told me that a Sunday beggar is a man who you let come for a warm meal to your house every Sunday. When the lunch was over my friend pek took me out to show me their Sunday beggar, who so obligingly had entertained us during our meal with his zither. He was sitting on the last step leading to their long, wooden verandah, playing his zither, an oldfashioned string instrument, frequent in Central Europe, especially in Austria. It is a shallow, square box with metal wires stretched across it and when they are plucked with a plectrum they produce a sweet but rather faint sound. This beggar, the pek told me, was an itinerant beggar who travelled all over Croatia and Slovenia, and sometimes even farther on, to Austria; but whenever he came to Zagreb, he knew that pek Vdović and his wife would give him a warm welcome and a meal. It was the only time I have seen a Sunday beggar.

The visit to Tkalčićeva stirred up other memories. It was on this street that I once came across a man, a self-styled painter, with his easel placed in the middle of the street, in front of one of the houses built in the modest Baroque so characteristic of Tkalčićeva street. He was so absorbed in his work that he did not notice me approach him from behind. As I did so I could read on a small card tucked at the corner of his easel - Matija Pokrivka, painter of the old and

Zagreb, Tkalčićeva, "Zagorka"

of the new Zagreb. He was a worker in some factory, he told me, and had taught himself to paint, as a hobby.

As such memories crossed my mind my eyes caught sight of a strange figure, a statue of a matronly woman dressed in the style of the late 19th century, with an umbrella in one hand, standing on a small patch of green grass, just in front of the house of my late friend pek Vdović. I immediately recognized her - it was Marija Jurić, the popular Zagorka, the authoress of the Witch from Grič, which had made her famous. I, too, was among the readers who had eagerly bought the next installment of her serial novel. Her book was looked down upon by more refined readers and the high-brow intellectuals, but I greatly enjoyed reading about the adventures of the two principal characters, the countess Nera

Zagreb, Kaptol

and the brave officer Siniša, the representatives of uprightness and goodness, persecuted by the evil forces.

Marija Jurić (1873 - 1957), who wrote under the penname of Zagorka, was the first woman professional journalist in Croatia, and a chronicler of old Zagreb. She wrote a number of novels among which the Witch from Grič is the most popular. The great popularity of this novel is based on the fact that Zagorka was concerned with the most important aspects of society of the time, and her characters fought against social injustice and the discrimination of women. She also wrote about the Croatian aristocracy, alienated from their own people and their national identity.

We continued our walk and as we passed one side-walk cafe after another I thought with nostalgia of Tkalčićeva from days gone by, as I remember it. A peaceful and out-of-the way street where children chased each other and played hopscotch, and where the most likely people to be seen were the local inhabitants. Revisiting the places dear to you often brings more disappointment than anticipated pleasure. They remained unchanged, fixed in our mind, and cannot come to our expectations any more. We resent the intrusion of inevitable changes dictated by exigencies of everyday life. We stopped at the point where Tkalčićeva ends and where Kaptol, Nova Ves and Zvonarnička (Sacristan's) Street meet, all sites dear to my eyes . At one corner stands a small chapel dedicated to St.Dimbuš, a strange name of an even stranger saint, apparently one of the robbers who was crucified with Christ, at least that is what I was once told by my friend Marija Strižić. On the other side stands the Kaptol elementary school to which my daughter went for two years, from 1948 to 1950. This is the oldest school in Croatia, as you can read on the plaque placed in 1985 on the occasion of the 150th anniversary. Miroslav Krleža, the well-known Croat writer had been one of its pupils, too. Strangely enough, my daughter had only faint memories of the school. She took some snapshots and thus we ended our tour on that day. A little rhyme kept coming back to my mind:

> *Na Kaptolu starom jedna škola stoji,*
> *Stopedeset ljeta ona već broji...*
> On the old Kaptol stands a school
> Which counts a hundred and fifty years...

The Manček Philharmonic Evenings

Revisiting old friends is an experience in which reality usually falls short of expectations. The distance and spans of time that separate us are not easily surmounted in spite of genuine efforts on both sides. However, old memories of shared events help somehow to fill the gap, and we carry on our conversation at first in a somewhat stumbling and halting manner to gradually regain former confidence and even intimacy. That is how it was on my former visits to Zagreb while I still lived in Yugoslavia.

This was my first visit to Zagreb since 1991, when Yugoslavia ceased to exist, after war broke out between the Yugoslav Army and the Croats who had proclaimed their independence. Things changed rapidly and radically after that, largely because of the rebel Serbs in the Krajina in Croatia, who caused a lot of trouble demanding and fighting for their autonomy. As a consequence,the animosity towards Serbs and everything connected with them was running very high among Croats. The war in Croatia could leave nobody untouched, against our wishes we found ourselves in two hostile and antagonistic camps.

Some of my oldest friends did not hesitate to let me know what they thought of Serbs, which was far from flattering, and one even went so far as to tell me that I had better not ever call her again. Bearing all this in mind, it is not surprising that I felt somewhat apprehensive at the thought of encountering even those friends who had responded to my letters from America in which I had announced our visit to Zagreb. It was certainly considerate, but nevertheless embarassing that when we did meet all of them carefully avoided mention of any political topics; and our conversation ranged from exchanging family news to other similar and neutral subjects. Only once, talking on the phone to a very dear friend of mine, during a long conversation which inevitably led to a discussion of the war did we touch upon the presentday situation in former Yugoslavia. It is a theme that you really cannot avoid because it so painfully infringes upon our lives. We disagreed on this political conflict. She objected to my saying that the Croats did not sufficiently take into account the Serbian point of view, and that they were not informed about the suffering of the Serbian population in those areas of Croatia and Bosnia engulfed by the war. Leaving apart politics both Croats and Serbs have suffered in this war and both sides bear their share of responsability for what is happening. I could not help feeling a kind of controlled tension that prevented us from being relaxed as we used to be in former days. The dinner at the home of a childhood friend of mine from Tuzla (who is Jewish) was another opportunity to hear a different view of the new regime in Croatia. We heard about massive corruption by those who are now in power, and who view the ethnic problem from an extreme nationalist perspective. Such nationalism has created intolerance and hatred towards the Serbs in Croatia and, in general, toward the former, supposedly Serb-dominated, Yugoslavia.

One of my daughter's schoolfriends, who came to see us in the hotel, was sincere and young enough to say about the Serbs what she had probably had heard from her parents, or close friends, and what may well be the view held by many Croats. She said that the Serbs had brought the Croats nothing but primitivism, cultural destruction, and brutal force, using the word "boot" as a metaphor for it.

Meeting old friends is a gratifying but emotionally and physically exhausting experience. After a few first visits I begin to feel both mental and physical fatigue. Constant and intense effort to communicate and in a short time to make up for a long absence drains me of all energy. And as visit followed visit, my supply of energy decreased. And, on each visit I noticed evidence of physical and mental deterioration in my friends, which they, no doubt, also noticed in me. The comforting thought is that we all share together these rites of passage. Less comforting was the news of the deaths of certain dear, old friend, which stired old memories mixed with the disturbing and disquieting thoughts of the inevitable end.

Two of very dear old friends had died since I had last been in Zagreb. One of them was Marjan Dubsky, known among his friends as Mančo. I thought with some concern of his wife Mira, who had invited us to lunch.

The Dubskys were among my oldest friends in Zagreb. Our friendship had never been too close, but we cultivated it at a comfortable distance, which made each encounter pleasant and refreshing despite the differences that existed in our temperaments and ways of life. I have always liked the orderly atmosphere of their old-fashioned home, full of period furniture, paintings and bibelots collected through generations. My favourite was a statue of St. Vaclav - Wenceslas -, who in the nineth century converted Czechs to Christianity, a reminder that Mančo's parents were Czechs and came to live in Zagreb before World War One, when Croatia was still part of Habsburg's Empire. In the past we played bridge together, and I always enjoyed being part of their big annual party given on Štefanje, the second day of Christmas, when almost all of their friends gathered together, making for a very large party. But what I will always remember them for is Mančo's passion for music, to which he devoted the greater part of his leisure time. He was a true and well-informed lover of music, and over many years he had collected an impressive number of records, which he willingly shared with his friends. He organized musical evenings known as Mančo's Philharmonic, and at the beginning of each season Mančo would send invitations to his friends with a full programme for the coming year. I have saved his invitation for the opening of the 38th concert season. It reveals Mančo's very fine sense of humor; it runs as follows:

"Your Lordship!"

The Management of the MančEk Philharmonic Orchestra has the honour of inviting you to the opening of the 38th concert season to be held on 3 October, 1968, at 8:30 p.m. On this occasion Antonin Dvorak's Requiem for soloists, choir and the orchestra will be performed. The concerts will be given every Thursday at 8:30 p.m. until 26 June, 1969. The most distinguished soloists and conductors from all countries will take part in the concerts. Special commemorations will be given on the occasion of the 75th anniversary of the death of P.I. Tchaikovsky (5 evenings), the 100th anniversary of the death of A.S. Dargomissky, the 100th anniversary of the death of H. Berlioz, and the 125th anniversary of the birth of N.A. Rimsky-Korsakoff. In addition to that a series of first-night performances will take place, among others the VI Symphony by A.Bruckner, the Symphony of Psalms by I.Stravinsky, Gloria by F. Poulenc, the III Symphony by G. Mahler, the Variations and Fugue on a theme of Mozart, and the Ballet Suite for orchestra by M.Reger, the Burlesque by Richard Strauss.

We hope that this season, too, you will be among our regular concert-goers.

Very respectfully,
The Management of the
Manček Philharmonic Evenings

Zagreb is a town with a long-established musical tradition, and the concerts given by the Zagreb Symphony Orchestra at Glazbeni Zavod (the Academy of Music), often featuring the world-renowned Solisti di Zagreb, or at the Istra were well-attended by a very discriminating audience. Mančo's Philharmonic evenings were only one among many examples of the high standards of musical culture attained by its inhabitants. Mančo lived long enough to celebrate the 50th anniversary of his Philharmonic, of which I was duly informed by an invitation to attend, but I was not able to come.

For many years my sister and I had spent the winter months in Opatija, and one of the principal pleasures I looked forward to was meeting there my old friends from Zagreb , Mančo Dubsky among them. The last time we had met there in the cafe of our Belvedere Hotel was shortly before Yugoslavia's demise , and I had not seen him after. I remember Mančo with pleasure, for he was a fine gentleman; somewhat reserved, he kept a pleasant silence in company while quietly smoking his pipe, and speaking only if directly addressed. And, of course, I shall remember him for his Philharmonic evenings.

A Ghost Story from the Upper Town

On a Sunday afternoon, several years ago, I went with Margit Miholić, a Swedish lady who had married a Croat, to visit her friends Misses Čučković. I was curious to meet them, for Margit often spoke of them, and from the way she discribed them I expected to be introduced to two anachronistic and excentric elderly ladies. I knew that they lived in Visoka ulica (the High Street), the oldest part of the Upper Town which in turn is the oldest part of Zagreb. They remained unmarried all their life and were now living in retirement. The elder sister taught history and was domineering over her yunger sister who was a schollar with two doctor's degrees, and was a librarian at the University Library.

To reach Visoka Ulica from Svibovac we had to pass through some very picturesque parts of Zagreb. We first crossed Nova Ves, a quiet street with respectable houses of retired deans and other ecclesiastics, and came to Tkalčićeva, one of the streets that still retains some of the charm of the old Zagreb. Its unpretentious houses are quite old, dating from the end of the 18th century. They are mostly homes of various artisans, and their wooden balconies and verandahs display pots of blooming geraniums and similar flowers. Children play in the street while cats sit on window sills and watch passers-by. A Hundred Steps, known also as Felbinger's Steps, lead from Tkalčićeva to the Upper Town. I have once made a point to count these steps and to my surprise found that there are about two hundred of them. An oddity in their name I cannot account for.

The Upper Town, always very quiet, was even more so because it was Sunday. We passed through its almost deserted streets,the Jelačić palace with its classical facade and the old park, formerly the residence of that noble family, but nowadays serving as a playing ground for children. We proceeded through Demetrova, a narrow, winding and slightly steep street, which brought us to number 6 in Visoka Street. We entered a simple courtyard through a small side gate. The main, large gate, formerly used for carriages, no longer in use stood locked. On the left side of the court was a modest-looking story house, and in front of us stood the house in which the Čučković sisters lived. It was quite simple but with that certain look of very old Upper Town houses that were changed and added to so often in the course of the years that it has become difficult to decide what style they belonged to. We climbed a flight of very old wooden steps and rang the bell. The door was opened by the elder Miss Čučković, a distinguished-looking elderly lady with grey hair and expressive, dark eyes. She must have been a great beauty in her young days, but now her thinness and a deep and sonorous voice somehow contrived to associate her in my mind with a picture of a virago.

We were admitted into a very pleasant drawing-room with two windows looking over a large stretch of the Tuškanac Forest and the Krleža house clearly in view on the other side of the Sophia's path (Sofijin put). There was another lady sitting in the room with a nervous little dachshund. He vigorously barked at us from under the settee which was placed in the middle of the room. The room did not have that crowded look so common in old houses where furniture has been ammassed through several generations, but made a pleasant impression of a place where there were no superfluous things. Walls were adorned with several diplomas in Latin and photographs of young women in old-fashioned dresses and hairdos, rather lovely to look at. There was a small chest-of-drawers with an Empire clock, ticking loudly, a very nice needle-work table, and some Biedermeier armchairs, so comfortable to sit in. Between the windows stood a small glass "vitrina" displaying all sorts of old porcelain cups and statues and other objects that people like to collect and display.

The old lady with the dachshund was Mrs.Dominis whose husband belonged to a very ancient family from the island of Rab. One of his ancestors was Markantun Dominis, a distinguished figure from the first half of the 17th century, about whom a play has been recently written (Heretik by Rudi Supek). He was a Jesuit who withdrew from the order to fight against the secular power of the Pope. He was persecuted by the Inquisition, and after his death his body, together with his books were burned in Rome, at the same place where Giordano Bruno had been burned alive before him. During his life he was for some time in England of James I, where he was appointed the Dean of Westminster. It was interesting to learn that he was in Shakespeare's London and knew England at the most interesting point of her history.

Soon the younger Miss Čučković came out of another room accompanied by a gentleman from the University Library who had come to consult her on some points she was particularly well informed about. She was as different from her rather beautiful and haughty sister as can be. Dressed in an old-fashioned and long grey dress, with her hair gathered into a big knot on the neck, she spoke very little, and impressed me as rather shy and diffident. Margit told me that the elder sister, Martha, often said that she could have married several times if it had not been for her younger sister Dana.

Our conversation turned round several topics of general interest. The afternoon was stormy with gusts of wind and rain, and as it slowly turned into the evening a light mist began to gather over Tuškanac forest, which was rather pretty. A perfect setting for ghost stories we actually shortly turned to.

It was Martha who began speaking about an old acquaintance of hers who was known to be very active and energetic in spite of her advanced age of eighty four. Her sister lived in Potkoren, a small town in Slovenia near the Austrian border. She had broken her leg and had to be treated at the hospital in Ptuj. As she had left her home in a hurry, without being able to put everything in order, she asked her sister Sida (for that was the name of the brave old lady) to come to the hospital to visit her as soon as possible. There she gave her the keys of her house, asking her to take her money and jewelry out of the drawer and keep it until she is well enough to return to her home where she lived all by herself. Sida (which is a short form of old-fashioned Sidonia) left immediately and went to her sister's house to do as she was told. She found everything in its proper place, put the money and the jewelry into a box, and placed it on a small table in the bedroom, and then she got ready to spend the night there. Before going to bed she wanted to make sure that the house was properly locked, and went once more downstairs in order to check the door. It was safely locked, and Sida climbed back to her room and went to bed. Before long she imagined to have heard some steps, and she began to listen attentively. There was no doubt, somebody was climbing the steps, and even more ominously the steps were drawing nearer and nearer to her room. As she was gazing from her bed frozen with fear the door knob slowly turned and the door opened quietly. In the darkness of the night she could percieve a figure all dressed in white standing for a moment at the door and looking at her.She plucked all her courage and said as confidently as she could manage:

Who are you ? Please, let me alone, and go away.

To her surprise the spectre began to advance and answered:

Do not be afraid. I mean no harm. You must by no account move from your bed, for if you do something terrible will happen to you.

Sida, while engaged in that strange conversation was keeping an eye on her box that stood between them. She admitted that even though she believed she was visited by a ghost she could not help thinking of her sister's money and jewelry now under her care.

As it happened, their younger brother who lived in Germany had died only several months before, and she was convinced that it was his spirit that was haunting her now. As she was obviously quite distressed the ghost repeated that she should not fear him, and that everything would be all right provided she promised not to leave her bed, and to make under no circumstances any noise. She was to leave the house quietly in the morning, he insisted, and to tell nobody a single word about having seen a ghost.

There was nothing for Sida but to promise it, and then the ghost said that he would make her some coffee in the kitchen, for she was so obviously in need of it. However, he repeated again, she must at no cost leave the bed. When the ghost disappeared downstairs, Sida quickly jumped out of her bed, took the box from the table and put it under the pillow. She was in bed when the ghost reappeared with a coffee tray, reproaching her for having walked in the room while he was in the kitchen. He said he could distinctly hear her walking, and poor Sida took great pains to persuade him that she had not done so. Then the ghost said that he would leave her, and asked her once more to talk to nobody about what she had seen and what had happened to her during the night. Before leaving her he said that he had his accomplices both here and in Zagreb, and if she did not keep her word something dreadful would befall her. She gave every possible promise, and clutching to her treasure under the pillow she spent the rest of the night very uncomfortably, turning over her thoughts and forebodings.

The house remained quiet for the rest of the night, and if it had not been for the tray with the Turkish coffee that was standing by her bed, she might believe she had only dreamed about it. Early in the morning she left the haunted house and took a bus for Zagreb. On her way there a man approached her and offered to carry her little bag, in which she had packed the money and the jewelry. She was scared to death believing that it was one of the ghost's accomplices.

She firmly gripped her little bag and muttered that it was not heavy at all. During the ride and upon the arrival in Zagreb she was imagining that she was followed, so she got off the tram a few stops before her street, and took a long, roundabout way home. When she was finally safely locked in her flat, she decided not to go out for several days, during which time she lived on practically nothing, a few biscuits, tea and some fruit that was left over before her journey to Slovenia.

She did not see anybody and did not breathe a word, wondering what would come out of it all, when one day somebody rang her bell and a strange woman asked to be admitted into the flat. Sida was convinced that it was one of the Ghost's Zagreb accomplices, and did not want to let her in, but the woman smiled very pleasantly and said that she had come to set her mind at peace. She then told Sida that she should no longer fear the Potkoren ghost. The ghost in effect was an acquaintance of hers, who was hiding in the empty house with his mistress, with whom he was planning to escape across the border to Austria. When they had realized that somebody was in the house, they got afraid they might be discovered, and eventually turned over to the police. They quickly made up their mind to scare and prevent whoever it was from finding them out. As they were now safely on the other side of the border there was no longer need for Sida to live in fear, and she was sent to tell her so.

Now Mrs.Dominis took the turn to tell a ghost story. It involved her husband who, she claimed, had extra sensory perceptivity that enabled him to see and predict events from his dreams or otherwise. Once he dreamt of a man who appeared naked and dripping with water at the door of his bathroom, silently making a sign towards the window under which stood an old stone well in their garden. A few days later they read in the newspapers that a horrible murder was discovered in a village not far from Zagreb. The victim was a young man who was drowned in the well by his mother and sister, who conspired to take over his part of the inheritance.

When her husband was still a young man living with his parents at the island of Rab, he came one day shivering to his mother and said he could not sleep in his bed because there was a putrifying body of another man lying there. His parents, shocked out of their wits, ran to his room and, of course, could not see anybody. They thought it was all some sort of an insipid joke on his part, but the boy was genuinely agitated, so they did not insist on his sleeping in his bedroom for that night. However, a day or so afterwards, a body of one of his teachers, who was drowned at sea, was discovered already in the state of decomposition.

We thought it quite extraordinary, and Mrs.Dominis provided an interesting explanation. She said she thought that in both instances the men at the moment of their death wanted their plight to be known, and her husband captured the message with his sensitive mind. Their old house in Demetrova 3 was known to be haunted by ghosts of several servants, who were believed to have been poisoned by the food cooked in the copper vessels. That happened a long time ago, and she said that Mr.Dominis's grand-mother told her that they were hastily buried in the cellar of the building. In spite of that, rumours about it spread, and peasants from the neighbourhood were ready to take revenge on the family when it was all hushed down. Still, the house is believed to be haunted by their spirits. Mrs. Dominis told of the time her husband went to the cellar, used partly as a wine cellar, and after digging for a short while discovered a skull and several bones. His grandmother asked him to put the bones to rest from where he had taken them. Dear Dana said that she has also known that the ghosts were "spooking" round the house. She actually used the term "špukati" which I have never heard before. It reminded me of Spook, the little Halloween ghost that my grandson Robert impersonated for the first time last year at Anchorage, Alaska, with his little sister Elizabeta dressed as a witch. I have a darling picture representing them in disguise holding two paper bags full of little "treats" given by the "freightened" and obliging neighbours.

The Wooden Kurija in Turopolje

The Wooden Kurija in Turopolje

One part of the Sava valley, to the south of Zagreb and in the close vicinity of the town itself, is known as Turopolje. Its strange name has always intrigued me as to its origin and meaning though never enough to make me look it up. Thus, it was left to a chance visit to the village of Lomnica to reveal details about this somewhat forsaken but charming part of Croatia.

One fine autumn Sunday, while returning from lunch at the Čatež Spa, my friend Ana Ibler suggested that we pass by the small village of Lomnica in Turopolje on our way to Zagreb. The reason for this detour was to pay a visit to the two Bedeković sisters who lived there in their old family house. I remember that they were occasionally mentioned among our friends, and what I had heard made me curious about them, but, I had never had the opportunity to meet them because they led a very secluded life. I was, therefore, very pleased at the thought that I was finally going to meet them.

They were maternal aunts of my old friend Dragica Perak, and having remained unmarried they had spent all their life together. We remembered a funny little detail about them spread by some malicious gossips from the Upper Town. According to it after their sister's death, when the inheritance was divided, the family insisted on treating them as one person on account of their being identical twins. But, this may be one of those stories that people are so fond of repeating, even though they know they are not based on facts but on mere fancy, if for no other reason than that they are too good to be ignored.

But, Bedeković twin sisters led a sufficiently unusual life-style for their time to justify their being viewed as eccentric. They were exceptionally well educated for girls born in the second half of the 19th century. Vilma had finished conservatory, and the other twin, Milka, studied painting in Munich at the same time as the famous Croatian painter Miroslav Kraljević. She spent a few months painting in Paris, which was quite an extraordinary thing for her time. She painted all her life and from time to time exhibited her paintings in a small gallery in the Upper Town. Later on in their life they both taught embroidery and fine needlework at a secondary school, and after they had retired they spent most of their time at Lomnica, where they raised chickens, kept dogs and cats, and cultivated their own vegetable garden.

As we did not know the right way to Lomnica we took the road to Velika Gorica, and on several occasions made inquiries about the village. After a number of false starts, we finally managed to get there, but still had to ask directions to the Bedeković "kurija", homestead. At long last our car stopped by the side of an old wooden fence through which we could see a rather neglected garden with a huge linden-tree in the middle, and the Bedeković kurija behind it. It was a one-story wooden house with a small balcony above the entrance gate, and a very high roof covered with old tiles. What we were looking at was a charming and quaint survival from the past, which Djalski so nostalgically evoked in his stories Under the Old Roofs. A huge lilac tree on the one side of the house, and an old wild rose bush on the other, all covered with bright red rosehips, spoke of the loving care of former inhabitants of this house. A huge weeping-willow tree spread its long, yellow sprigs to the very ground covered with soft grass. The house and everything around it was so quiet that it gave the impression of a mirage or of a dream. We crossed the garden and gently pushed the door of the house, over which the year 1830 was distinctly inscribed. It gave way at the slightest touch, for it was only half closed. As our eyes adapted to the darkness reigning in the small hall, we gradually began to distinguish the contours of an old coach, which occupied the central place in it. Its black leather roof was well pulled over as if to protect its former occupants from the sun or from the rain. A charming vestige of days long gone by when a horse-drawn carriage was the only means of transportation. And a touching way of recognizing and repaying the services rendered. Other objects were looming about in the darkness, among others a well-preserved home brandy still. It was strange that we did not spot it before, because the hall was permeated with a strong smell of fermentation. Also, I don't know why we at first failed to notice the steps leading upstairs, unless it was because they were partly hidden behind the roof of the coach. And so, we quietly left the hall and went out in the hope of finding some other way to get to the upper floor. Our search was fruitless, all we could see were several hens quietly pecking in the yard behind the house. No other signs of life were visible, but we did not want to give up yet. I looked up and noticed an open window adorned with some flower pots, and with a piece of cloth fluttering in the breeze. Those were welcome signs, for it looked after all as if somebody must be living here. To my "Anybody home?" a faint response came from somewhere inside the house. We returned to the hall and at the same time we heard light steps coming down the stairs behind the coach. The next moment a tall, thin elderly lady was standing before us. It was one of the Beděković twin sisters smiling at us. I introduced myself and Ana, and told her that we were good friends of their niece Dragica Perak, adding that we would very much like to pay them a visit and see something of their old home, of which we had heard so much.

Upstairs we met the other twin sister, who was just as thin and fragile. They were unbelievably alike, almost identical. Dressed in the simple, long dark-blue dress with tiny white polka dots, their white hair done in an old-fashioned bun at the top of their head, they seemed to have come from another world and time, totally in keeping with their old house. They both had the same bright, china-blue eyes that smiled at us all the time we were talking. Very pleased with our visit, we were soon talking about my father-in-law, the late dr.Tomislav Tomljenović, and his wife, Minka Domac who belonged to the old Zagreb families, which they knew so well.

We were sitting in the drawing-room, called the "palača", full of all kinds of furniture, indiscriminately accumulated through many years, and overflowing with knick-knacks, most of them from the end of the last century. China plates and faiance jugs and pots filled every bit of free space on the shelves, and an equal number of vases of uncertain provenance were displayed on various chests and tables. The door of the small wooden balcony that we had seen above the entrance gate was wide open, offering us a picture perfect view of the old park in its autumn glory. Through the branches of the trees we could see part of the Lomnica river quietly flowing just beside the road in front of their house with a flock of white ducks happily swimming in it. We were sitting around a massive oak table in the middle of the room, with an old oil lamp suspended above it. When we expressed our admiration for it, the sisters hastened to demonstrate to us that it was provided with an electric bulb. I noticed a solitary swallow's nest attached to one of the beams in the ceiling, but without birds. It was late in the autumn and they had all gone to warmer regions. Family portraits of close and of more distant relatives gloomily looked down upon us from every wall, many of them painted by one of the twin sisters. Among these portraits two elaborate and impressive family trees occupied the place of honour. The sisters told us how long and how hard they worked at them over many years. They first spent a lot of time consulting family papers and searching parish archives, and then, during long winter evenings and nights they patiently pieced together the data they had thus collected. They obviously felt great satisfaction at seeing the result of their labours, and thought that they were sufficiently rewarded for their efforts with all the material they had assembled, for it was valuable not only to their families, but to other more distantly related people.

They told us that the wooden house in Lomnica was built by Petar pl. (plemeniti, of noble birth) Modić, their maternal great-grandfather. The fact has been recorded on a wooden beam and runs as follows: *Fieri facit Petrus Modich 1806.*

It struck me as interesting that among the portraits and other paintings there were several representing Napoleon or some episodes from his life. I was thinking about asking how those pictures found their way to Lomnica, but an opportune moment never presented itself. Perhaps an ancestor was an admirer of the Emperor, or perhaps there was another explanation for the conspicuous place that Napoleon had been accorded in this strange house. I was particularly arrested by the painting with Napoleon in a troyka wildly driven across the grim and snowbound Russian steppes, probably during the fateful retreat from Moscow. It was in such an odd contrast with this peaceful and pastoral environment.

We were instead shown an old armchair which, the sisters claimed, was covered with doormouse skins. How many doormice had to be caught in order to cover this dilapidated armchair, I silently wondered, but took their word for it. When I later asked Dragica about that armchair, she dismissed it with a laugh as a humbug and a family legend, the origin of which she was not able to account for.

The autumn days being short, we began to think of taking our leave for it was rapidly getting dark. One of the sisters saw us off to the car and stood there for a while talking to us, as though she was reluctant to let us go. It was the first and the last time that I had seen them, and I shall always remember them as they were on that autumn Sunday afternoon in their wooden house in Lomnica. I heard from Dragica that this house was subsequently declared a cultural monument, and is now in the charge of the Regional Institute for the protection of cultural and historical monuments. Everything in it and around it will be preserved exactly as it looked when the the Bedeković sisters lived there.

And what about Turopolje?

Its name keeps the memory of the distant past when herds of European wild bulls, aurochs, which are related to American bizon, roamed across the vast Pannonian Plain. In the archaic Slav language this animal was called tur, and the name Turopolje simply means aurochs' field, despite the fact that their breed had long been extinct. However, even today cattle-breeding is an important branch of economy in these parts. The Turopolje breed of pigs is well known and is equal to that from Yorkshire and the Netherlands.

But Turopolje is distinguished for yet another and quite different reason. This fertile valley has been inhabited since time immemorial. In the 13th century the Hungarian-Croatian King Bella IV confered the title of nobility upon several families from Turopolje for the services rendered to him. The legend has it that it was done in recognition of their sheltering the king during the Tartar invasion when he sought refuge in Turopolje. He had hid in a strong castle there, and they brought him branches loaded with succulent plums on which he survived. Hence the slightly derogatory term of "šljivari" (plum nobility) was attached to the families to whom Bella IV confered the title. For many centuries the inhabitants of Turopolje fought battles against the Bans and other feudal lords to preserve their privileges. By the end of 19th century "the noble community of Turopolje" became equal to other parts of the country. But the descendants of the noble families of "šljivari" – small landed gentry – still cherish the memory of the former glory of Turopolje.

Trnovec Rivisited, – or –
The Copelius from Hrvatsko Zagorje

As we drove through the wintry countryside, barely frosted with snow, memories emerged of my former visits to Trnovec, many years ago, and I felt a keen anticipation at the thought of revisiting it again. Ana and I have just left the Varaždin Arboretum, where we have picked some greenery for Christmas decoration, and on the spur of the moment have decided to pay a visit to Trnovec. We were hoping to see our friend Pucika Andrassy, who spends most of her weekends there.

Trnovec is a small family estate with a charming old house, passed down by her maternal family. It lies in Hrvatsko Zagorje, not far from Krapina, the site where the remains of the prehistoric Neanderthal man were discovered. Hrvatsko Zagorje is a region of a great natural beauty. It is dotted all over with lovely mansions and gracious castles, slumbering peacefully amidst their old, neglected parks, dreaming perhaps of days long past, when feudal lords still used to live there. The gently rolling hills are covered with hamlets and a patchwork of small plots of cultivated land, orchards and vineyards, on which the former serfs have toiled for centuries and as a result have given the Zagorje a well-groomed and civilized appearance of a big park. The descendents of those serfs are today the landowners, while the descendents of former feudal lords are no longer masters, nor do they, on the whole, own their former manors and castles. Thus, a certain justice has been finally achieved in bringing these two antagonistic groups into a harmonious coexistence.

Small chapels are perched on almost every hill, and weatherbeaten, bleached crucifixes stand forlornly by the side of dusty country roads. Once, I have seen a procession of pious pilgrims, "Romari" as they are called here, going on the pilgrimage to the ancient shrine of the miracle-working Holy Mother of God of Bistrica, Marija Bistrička. As they slowly went along they prayed and chanted:

> *Majko Božija Bistrička,*
> *Smiluj se na nas...*
> (Holy Virgin of Bistrica,
> Have mercy upon us...)

It was a strangely medieval sight, all those peasants, old and young, healthy and ill, most of them barefoot, with faces transfigured in the firm belief that their various problems and illnesses will be miraculously healed.

I have often thought that Hrvatsko Zagorje might have easily been the place where the grim fairy tale of Hansel and Gretel had taken place. During the feudal times peasants here lived in great poverty, which drove them in dispair to organise an uprising against their cruel lords. It was led by a legendary leader, Matija Gubec, but the revolt was crushed in a terrible bloodbath. However difficult it is to imagine parents abandoning their children in a forest to solve their food shortage problem, the very existence of such a fairy tale serves as a proof that such cases must have actually occurred. It was perhaps because of that poverty and hunger in times past that "kumeki", peasants from Zagorje, have never been credited with much intelligence, and have often been referred to as "bedasti", dumb and credulous, without that natural shrewdness that is traditionally ascribed to peasants from other parts of our country.

There is a charming and very popular song to that effect, in which Jankec, a simple-minded young peasant from Zagorje, goes to Zagreb to sell his farm produce at the market. He is in no hurry to catch the train, which is just about to leave, and when his friends urge him to run, he goodnaturedly replies:

Let it go, it does not matter, for I have the ticket in my pocket.

I would take the same, slow passenger "Zagorec" train that runs between Zagreb and Rogatec, and stops at every small station to collect peasants carrying chicken and famous Zagorje turkeys together with other good things to the Zagreb market. I would get off at Velika Ves, and then follow the road leading to Krapinske Toplice, the Krapina Spa, and it would bring me to Trnovec after a leisurely walk of only two kilometres.

So far as Pucika Andrassy knows, Trnovac has been their property for the last 350 years, and has come to her through her grandfather, baron Kosta Rukavina, who in turn had inherited it from his mother, countess Keglević. At the time when I first started coming to Trnovec, her father, Imbro plemeniti (of noble birth) Igalffy lived there, all by himself, a life of an utter excentric and recluse. Already at first sight he struck me as being like nobody else that I knew, but I am prepared to admit that this impression might have been partly coloured by what I had heard about him before our meeting. He was then an old man, and despite his fragile frame gave the impression of health and vigour. He always seemed to wear hunting clothes that appeared to be of a Tyrolian type. I remember that his coat buttons were made of stag's antlers. There was something decidedly old-fashioned about him, including his short, pointed beard. But, by far the most arresting were his pale-blue eyes, which seemed to me to be invested with an iron determination. He was one of the most relentless and passionate shots, huntsmen and taxidermists, and had spent all his life in the pursuit of these activities. It would be impossible to say how many animals he had killed and preserved during his lifetime. He was thought to hold the grim record of having killed and stuffed more animals than anybody else in Yugoslavia. Towards the end of his life he was awarded a Medal of the First Order for his hunting accomplishments of which he was extremely proud.

Imbro Igalffy has turned Trnovec into a regular natural science museum with a unique private collection of trophies, stuffed animals of all kinds, and cabinets with endless rows of boxes displaying butterflies and other insects from the region. The corridors and the walls of Trnovec were covered with plaques bearing antlers of all imaginable sizes and with animals in characteristic postures, each of them killed and artistically preserved by Mr. Imbro Igalffy's expert hands. You could see a lonely fox for ever lightly treading on top of a glass cabinet, which contained some similar animals in its shelves. A badger seemed to be just coming out of its lair, carefully sniffing the air, while a wild cat was fixed as it was preparing to jump off a branch. I particularly liked a big, black raven, thoughtfully sitting on the old piano in the messy drawing-room, full of antique and old-fashioned furniture and daguerreotypes representing ladies and gentlemen in hunting costumes, after the fashion prevailing in the period prior to the First World War. The raven is placed, very appropriately, in that room which is fraught with an atmosphere of days past, and whenever I looked at it I almost expected it to croak: Never more.

But, best of all I liked the delicate bats, suspended on a very thin, almost invisible piece of thread, so that they seemed to be floating and hovering under the old oil lamps, giving the weird impression of being alive whenever they were caught in the current of the air, which gently swung them to and fro.

Such was the strange and fascinating world in which Imbro Igalffy, like the old magician Copelius, reigned. There was something terrifying about this destructive passion of his, for he seemed to kill animals for the sheer pleasure of killing, as he kept on doing it regardless of the number of animals and insects he had already assembled in his very large collection. When Katarina became a biology student, Mr. Igalffy made her a present of several boxes of beautiful butterfly specimens, and she told me that they were preserved and presented more beautifully than some they had in their university collections. But, we both felt that a true lover of nature would protect rather than kill the animal life around him. Ironically, in the corridor of Trnovec there was a cupboard where Imbro Igalffy kept his bottles and other taxidermic paraphernalia with the inscription: *Wer liebt der lebt* – He who loves, lives.

But Imbro Igalffy was a passionate collector of many other things, especially those related to biology. Beside birds and animals, he collected skulls of animals, worms, snakes, birds' eggs, stones, plants and flowers, animal excrements, excavated objects, stamps, picture postcards, railway tickets, and God knows what else. In addition, he was a gentlemen-farmer and supported his family from the produce he grew on his land. He was also an accomplished cabinetmaker, for he had learnt the trade during his stay at Theresianum in

Vienna, and has adorned with old-fashioned woodcarvings their furniture at Trnovec.

When I came to Trnovec for the first time, Mr.Igalffy brought out their old guest-book, in which I had the pleasure of adding a few words to a long series of impressions and reflections that had been written in it before me by other visitors and friends over a period of many years. The guest-book was in perfect keeping with the antiquainted atmosphere of the whole place, so much so that in fact I would not have been surprised to find a similar book – *Spomenar* – an album, which was all the craze and fashion among the young ladies of several generations ago, lying on a table in their drawing-room. Such albums were full of improvised pieces of poetry, original or reproduced, and other accidental sayings, inscribed by young ladies' admirers, designed to prevent them from forgetting them.

Such thoughts and recollections flashed through my mind while Ana was struggling along the slippery country road, covered with the thin crust of frozen snow, which often caused our car to skid. We carefully drove through the gateway to Trnovec, between two square pillars made of brick, and had soon to abandon the car and proceed by foot. In the quiet of the winter day the old house stood on a small hillock among the trees, and with its windows hidden under the pale-blue wooden shutters it gave the impression of the Enchanted Castle, in spite of its outwardly modest appearence. Its simple, rectangular shape, its portico with a massive wooden door, its steep roof with the old tiles, all retained some vestiges of former dignity, which did not clash too much with its present somewhat delapidated looks. Covered with snow it was slumbering under the protection of four mighty spruce trees, and made you think of the Castle of the Sleeping Beauty, with which it has a very close resemblance, for Trnovec means a briar copse.

We entered by the service door into the small wooden gallery, an obvious addition to the original structure made to connect two separate parts of the old building. Pucika was in the room her father used to live in. She was talking to a peasant who had brought some cottage cheese for her.

Pucika is in her way even more excentric than her father was, trying to do the impossible – to divide her life between her home in Zagreb in the Upper Town in Opatička (Nuns' Street) and Trnovec manor in Zagorje. After her father's death she felt, perhaps more so than before, that it was now her duty to look after the land and the property, which Imbro Igalffy had cared for while he was alive. So she comes to Trnovec every weekend, where she labours growing potatoes and other vegetables for her family, although it would be much simpler and also more economical simply to buy them at the market. When the results of her work fall short of expectations, she is never discouraged, and undaunted, she starts it all over again the following season.

Pucika was dressed in an old tweed skirt and even older leather jacket that used to belong to her mother. She was very pleased to see us, and soon we were engaged in a lively conversation sitting round a massive Alt-Deutsch table. Before long, Ana and I began to freeze in spite of the wood fire merrily crackling in the big white tile stove. The house is no longer inhabited except when Pucika comes here in weekends, and takes a long time to warm up the thick, cold walls of the room in which she makes fire for herself.

Despite the bitter cold I went through all the rooms of Trnovec. The cold, stangant air cast a gloom that filled them up to their old, vaulted ceilings, and they appeared more desolate and deserted than ever. My old acquaintance, the raven, was still on the grand piano, and though I was pleased to see him, he somehow only intensified the gloomy atmosphere that was reigning in the rooms. Everything looked exactly as it did many years ago when I last was here. A strong smell of apples, gathered in their orchard and carefully stored in the hall, was lingering all over the house. Everything that I looked at reminded me of the late Imbro Igalffy. His horns were hanging on the walls, and I suspected that nobody will blow them again. The stags' antlers, closely arranged on the walls, looked like so many branches of a bare forest sunk in an endless dream.

My last recollections of Imbro Igalffy are not very pleasant. It was in the autumn of 1960, before Katarina had left for the University of Pennsylvania. We were at Trnovec for the week-end, and were getting ready to catch the train for Zagreb, while Mr. Igalffy and his younger grandson, Mladen, were out in front of the house. Suddenly they noticed and owl standing beside the chimney on the roof and Mr.Igalffy rushed into the house to fetch the gunds. Both Rina and I went out to see what was going to happen and our hearts sank when we saw the lovely bird peacefully sitting on the roof, completely unaware of its imminent doom. Mr. Iggalffy was giving the instructions to his grandson how to shoot, and at the same instant we heard the shot, and the owl noislessly tilted and fell to the ground. Mr. Igalffy grabbed it immediately, and while it was still warm began to skin it, telling us at the same time how he was going to preserve it. And there were already quite a few owls in his collection.

I have retained, however, some more pleasant memories from the same week-end. While Pucika was seeing us off, she suddenly remembered that we should take some cider with us. She took us into a nearby building where they kept an ancient, wooden wine press. It looked very large and crude, and I watched with great interest and amusement as Pucika applied all her strength to crane a big wooden handle, which in turn set into motion its elaborate mechanism. It gave off strange, creaking whirring sounds, as though reluctant to work, but eventually it produced some apple cider, which came out of a spout, somewhere at the far end of that prehistoric contraption.

As usual, Pucika complained of the cost of maintaining this property at Trnovec. She always thought that selling it to the state was the only solution. Then it could be properly refurbished and might be used as a tourist attraction, or as a summer camp for children, like so many other stately homes in Zagorje. I do not know why, but I always had the impression that Pucika only talked about it and secretly hoped that they would never sell Trnovec, so dear to her. Her own children were far too busy with their careers to devote enough time , energy or money to old Trnovec. Meanwhile, it was slowly but inevitably decaying.

Pucika asked Ana whether she would take an old suitcase, full of apples, to their home in Opatička. It was too heavy for us to carry it to the car, and so Pucika ran into their storage room to fetch a small sleigh. The amount of useless and discarded things accumulated there through years was simply staggering. Among other old objects I recognized with a pang of nostalgia an old rusted centrifuge for the extraction of honey, which made me remember Juraj's beekiping days after the war. Rina and I sometimes accompanied him to the country, where he kept his beehives.

Pucika pulled the sleigh with the heavy suitcase, well loaded with apples, and the three of us managed to push it into the trunk. We parted with Pucika, leaving her to her business -she had an appointment with a forester who was to mark out the trees she wanted to have cut down.

Soon, Trnovec and the strange world of Imbro Igalffy were behind us. I thought of him and of Lacek, an old servant of theirs whom I used to see during my former visits to Trnovec. He always struck me as an unusual man. His finely chiseled features and a narrow and distinguished nose were more appropriate for a gentleman than a peasant. When I once asked Pucika about him, she told me that Lacek was a natural son of her grandfather. And then she added that Lacek did not particularly care for women, but lived with men, an unexpected lifestyle in a peasant. Both Mr.Igalffy and Lacek are no more, but I believe that their ghosts still linger about Trnovec. And the stuffed birds Mr.Igalffy had shot, left to themselves are mouldering away, and much to Pucika's regret serve as an easy prey to mice, which now reign in the deserted Trnovec.

Opatija, park in the Belvedere Hotel

Opatija - Now and Then

From Zagreb we took a bus to Opatija, which we included in our itinerary when we were making plans for our visit to Yugoslavia.

The greater part of our ride to Opatija took us through the beautiful Gorski Kotar, an area covered with dense fir and beach forests, a home of bear, chamois and capricailles.

Opatija, Villa Rozalia, now Casino

Because of the exceptional features of its flora and fauna world, part of the Gorski Kotar – Risnjak – has been declared a national park.

We arrived in Opatija late in the afternoon. I was happy and moved to be once again in the Belvedere Hotel, where my sister Branka and I had spent our winter months for more than 15 years. Its lovingly tended park, its terrace with old pine trees and the view of Rijeka and the islands of Krk

Opatija, neglected park of Villa Irinea

and Cres across the bay looked unchanged. But much had happened since I last was here in 1991.

It was good to be received and treated as an old guest, and as such to accept little signs of attention, not the least being the chance to hear what some of the old waitresses, including a person at the reception desk, thought of the present situation. Their somewhat circumspect comments and remarks implied that things were not as they used to be, but they hoped for the best.

The hotel seemed to be quite full, guests were slowly coming back. The war in Croatia has done much damage to tourism. Guests from abroad were still reluctant to come to the Adriatic in the numbers that visited here before the war, but tourist trade will soon pull the Croatian economy out of the slump in which it is now languishing.

The dinner was far better than any dinner I could remember from former visits – fresh sea fish (before, we usually had frozen fish) with mangold and boiled potatoes in butter as the main course – all very well prepared.

Opatija – a big tourist centre and a health resort is in the eastern part of Istria at the foot of Učka mountain and the Gorski Kotar region. Unlike other towns on the Adriatic Coast, which have a long history, reflected in their architecture, Opatija sprang within a relatively short period of prosperity when it was still part of the Austro-Hungarian Empire. Its development into a tourist centre is associated with the construction of the Vienna-Trieste railway (1857), with a branch leading to Rijeka. This event made Opatija, until then a small fishing village in a sparcely populated area, accessible to the more distant parts of the hinterland. Its climate, which combines the balmy sea air with the fresh mountain air, and its beautiful location soon attracted people of consequence from Austria, and in particular from Vienna, whose counts and barons sought repose and recovery from bustle and noise of this European metropolis.

Many years have gone by since then bringing many changes in their wake, but the place still retains the appearance its builders had given it. It bears the stamp of time in which it was created, between the two centuries, when the Secession was at its height. Most of the houses and hotels built at that time have been preserved almost unchanged until today. With their white stucco floral patterns on the pastel facades of the hotels and villas decked with wrought iron balconies and fences, they provide a veritable parade of the good specimens of Art Nouveau.

There was a time when Opatija, or Abbazia as it was then called, was an exclusive, smart seaside resort, where the cream of the Austrian and Hungarian society gathered together. However, the era of aristocracy and bourgeoisie was superseded by the era of the proletarians after World War Two. Opatija was then beleaguered by the people from all parts of our country who could afford, during a short period, to stay in these lovely hotels because they could pay by the coupons obtained from the trade unions. Most of them happily walked past these testimonials of the Secession without having ever heard of it.

View of Volosko

The following morning I took Katarina for a walk along the seashore, "lungo mare", a path that stretches from Volosko to as far as Lovran on the other end of the bay. It serves as a pleasant promenade and constitutes the chief diversion for the visitors in the course of which they can enjoy lovely vistas of this part of the Opatija riviera.

I used to go along "lungo mare" almost every morning on my way to Volosko where I bought newspapers and cigarettes for my sister, or did some other errands. Early in the morning this path is still little frequented by visitors, so I had it almost all to myself. I always looked forward to the part of the walk where there are several old oak trees reaching almost to the very shore, and standing at some distance from each other as if guarding the path. Their twisted and gnarled roots clutch firmly to the rocks on which they grow making me think of some mythical dragons with scaly limbs and claws. There are also old gardens which surround the villas that once belonged to Austrian and Hungarian noblemen. Recently, most of these villas had been inhabited by people who had come to the seaside from all the various parts of Yugoslavia. Not only could they not afford to properly maintain them but, they distroyed them by arbitrarily altering the former architecture to suit their own needs. These gardens still retained some semblance of their former beauty in spite of the jungle-like state into which they had degenerated during a long period of neglect. I sometimes used one of them as a short cut to Volosko because I enjoyed walking through its overgrown paths. With its huge cypress trees and its old evergreen oak it seemed a fitting place for the statues of classical style of sylvan gods and goddesses. They, too, had fallen into decay, and with resignation looked upon the children who came to play in their abandoned garden.

The road to Volosko leads up a hill, for the old town was built above the little harbor and the sea. Old Volosko was the home of former sea captains, and of the geophysicist Andrija Mohorovičić, for whom a layer in the earth has been named. Today it has become part of Opatija and of its busy tourist trade. When you leave the main street you find yourself in a maize of crooked little streets and old houses provided with balconies and strange chimney-pots. Before entering Volosko we stopped for a moment to admire the lovely view of Quarnero Bay that stretched before us. There is an old house here standing in a small garden overgrown with rosemary bushes along its rusted iron fence. It used to belong to a sea captain, but today it has been divided among his descendants who live in it only in the summer. We plucked some rosemary sprigs to take home for their bitter-sweet scent and memories of our Dalmatian coast.

What I was told by refugees

During our short stay in Opatija I have learnt far more what people thought of the current situation in the country than I had in Zagreb. Some chance encounters with local people shed a little more light on what things looked like from their point of view. But the really interesting and authentic information about the new realities of life in Croatia came from total strangers through chance encounters.

While I was waiting for the bus for Medveja, where I wanted to visit an old friend from Zagreb, who spent part of the year in her villa there, I happened to stand close to two women who were waiting for the same bus. I immediately recognized them as refugees, for they did not look like the local people and even less like visitors. The elder woman was from Konjic; she said she had left her home to save herself from the Croats, and said that the Serbs had helped her to escape. The younger woman told a different story. She, too, was from Konjic, but she was obliged to flee from Serbian soldiers. They lived now in Lovran, together with other refugees from Bosnia. Some were in hotels, and some in private rooms, paid for by the Croatian government. On the bus I sat next to a woman from Labin, in Istria, and she talked about their everyday problems - the high cost of living, low incomes with the mounting inflation. She was very critical of the new government in Zagreb, whose members apparently were concerned only with getting better positions and spending government money freely. On my way back from Medveja I talked with a woman, a Croat refugee from Vukovar, who began her story by complaining about the local authorities who were in charge of the UN relief sent to refugees from abroad. She said they kept all the best things for themselves, leaving to the refugees what they themselves did not want. Then, she said, they sold those better things and made good money with which they bought elegant cars and even houses. The corruption became so rampant that it was eventually decided that all the things coming from abroad should be provided with a special seal so that they could not be sold any longer. I wanted to hear about Vukovar, the town which was all but destroyed during the fighting over it. I told her that I had seen on TV in Belgrade a picture of a line of tractors loaded with bedding and essential houshold things, among which sat members of a family, with the father as a driver. When the reporter asked them why and where they were going, the man said with resignation: "We don't know". The answer did not make sense and it puzzled me.

The woman from Vukovar threw quite a new light on that picture. She said that those people must have been the Serbs from the villages around Vukovar, or from Vukovar itself, who had been informed by the Yugoslav Army that they were going to attack Vukovar, and that they had better leave it at once if they wanted to save their lives. She added that those who refused to go, were moved by force, without much ceremony.

Our last and very interesting interview was with a street sweeper, a young man from Opatija. We began to talk to him while waiting in front of the Slavija Hotel for the bus from Pula, which was to take us back to Zagreb. We commended the cleanliness of Opatija, but the young street sweeper complained about the tourists and strangers who made it dirty. He added that few people wanted to clean streets nowadays, it was the kind of work much looked down upon. He was dressed in blue overalls, and all the time we talked to him he was holding his strange broom, used by street cleaners in Opatija. It was made of a spiky and prickly tuft of some Mediterranean plant. Soon after this neutral exchange we found ourselves talking politics, and he expressed his dissatisfaction with the economic and political situation in Croatia today. He said that here, in Istria, nothing remained to them, for all the money generated by the tourist trade went to the government in Zagreb. This remark sounded familiar to me and made me think of the eternal complaints made by Croats in former Yugoslavia. They, too, claimed that all the money from Croatia went to Belgrade, where they had no means to control the use it was put to. The young man went on to complain of the taxes imposed by the state so that people like him could hardly make ends meet. It sounded as if there was not much reason to be pleased with the order of things. It was interesting that he also had nothing nice to say about the Catholic church, a topic he introduced himself for some reason. He claimed that children could not be enrolled in elementary school if their priest did not confirm that they attended church services.

Clappers from Kastav Region

February is a month of carnivals, which are observed with particular enthusiasm along the Dalmatian coast. During the period of these festivities, popularly called "fashnik", Opatija assumes a new guise with all kinds of traditional celebrations, concerts and shows. The main street, always very lively with tourists and visitors, becomes packed with people from Opatija, Rijeka and other nearby or more remote places, all come to see or to take part in the carnival procession. At every vantage point improvised stands with *krafni* (doughnuts), or sausages cooked on the spot are sold to eager customers. Everybody is in a happy, carefree mood, laughing and talking at the top of the voice amidst the general hullabaloo.

Carnival processions are among the most popular, and local people participate in them with great enthusiasm, but visitors from Italy and Austria are often included in them as well. With their rich and glamorous costumes they far outshine those of domestic manufacture. In one thing, however, they cannot compete with us, and that is with our "zvončari", clappers, a fascinating relic and reminder of days gone by.

Only a few kilometres to the north of Opatija lies Kastavština – the Kastav region – in former days a cattlebreeding area. This kind of economy was closely associated with the custom of clapper processions. Today such processions form part of carnival festivites, but clapper processions have their roots in pre-Christian beliefs and magical performances. Originally, they were performed as an apotropaion – an act to drive away evil spirits at the end of winter, when the time of the new, fertile cycle was approaching. Clappers wore a mask, usually representing the head of an animal, and were wrapped up in sheep skins, carrying a mace in one hand, with one big or three small bells – clappers – hanging from their waists. A group of men dressed in such a costume would set out on fixed days to pass through their own and the neighbouring villages. After they had made a broad circle they would return to their own villages in the evening. In every village through which they passed, clappers performed a special dance during which they kept colliding with one another causing their clappers to produce a terrific din, and ending with a round dance. Everywhere, they were welcomed and offered food and drinks, after which they proceeded to the next village. During the two days that preceded Ash Wednesday some of the clappers carried a small sack filled with ashes which they scattered around during the toor of the villages – an old practice meant to invoke and ensure fertility. Clappers from the Kastav region were part of a widespread tradition encompassing other parts of Istria, regions in the Alps, and in many other parts of the Balkans.

Two Wild Swans

Spring, the sweet spring, is the year's pleasant king,
Then blooms each thing, then maids dance in a ring,
Cold does not sting, the pretty birds do sing
Cockoo, jug-jug, powe, towitta-woe.

– Thomas Nash

At the seaside in our country February is a month that brings constant changes and surprises. It is the month when the first messengers of spring begin to appear - overnight almond trees become decked in delicate, white blossoms, the crowns of daisies peep out of grass timidly by the side of the more aggressive, star-like dandelions, and the forests wake up from their winter hibernation. I like trees best when "still transparent to the view, the downy woods are greener-tinted", when young leaves are only just beginning to open, and when it is still possible to distinguish shades of pale russet, tawny and yellow colours of the different trees before they are engulfed by leaves. Every day when I went out for a walk I cast a glance towards the slopes of Učka and the adjacent Veprinac to feast my eyes on that miracle of spring. At Črnikovica, the highest point on the road to Volosko, I made a habitual stop. There, I had discovered and befriended a little, neglected garden in the midst of which stood an old, one-story house with all the shutters firmly closed. The house was uninhabited at this time of the year and appeared to be sunk in a sleep while all around it there was abundant evidence of new life. Slowly, I walked along the path overgrown with ivy and grass, feeling for a moment like the proprietor of this charming garden. Yellow, white and violet crocuses have already come out in one part of the garden, in another I notice a small tuft of daffodils under a magnolia tree covered in buds ready to burst out at any moment. Daffodils "which come before the swallow dares, and take the winds of March with beauty"- no doubt Shakespeare is right when he speaks of the English spring but to our Mediterranean parts spring comes earlier, in February. Old rosemary bushes growing along the corroded iron fence were already all covered with pale-blue flowers, and when I broke off a small twig and rubbed it into my hand its pungent, aromatic scent tickled my nose and my memory.

The sun was so hot that I felt uncomfortable in my winter coat. Lower down and farther away the sea was shimmering in the light morning mist, and the islands of Cres and Krk were outlined in the distance with many shades of blue colours. Everywhere there was light, warmth and colour. It was spring.

But, the weather changed quickly, overnight the south wind began to blow and howl driving dark clouds which brought rain and depression. The sea was agitated and its huge waves relentlessly broke against the embankment in front of our hotel. The mountains of the Gorski Kotar with their snow-capped ranges only yesterday glittering in the bright sunshine today were hidden in mist and clouds. Cres and Krk could no longer be seen while Učka and Veprinac with the steeple of its ancient church were also covered with thick fog. Everything was bleak and sad and we seemed to be in the midst of winter again, with little hope of the sun soon appearing. However, this spell of bad weather did not last long here. Good and bad weather here quickly succeed each other. After the recent cold and rain we were the more keenly appreciative of the clear sky, the sunshine and of the intensely blue sea, which so easily changed its moods. One day it roared and broke huge waves against the shore, the other it showed its serene and peaceful face. Visitors quickly reappeared, resuming their daily walks along "lungo mare", the coast path. Some were in groups, they were talkative and gay Italians; some walked in pairs, but many took solitary walks. Others sat on the benches sunbathing, or just resting watching the more active passers-by. "Young lovers meet, old wives a-sunning sit". Some things never change.

Like people, animals, too, seemed to seek their companions. The plump little blackbirds in the park of our hotel were very active, incessantly hopping along in search of food, often generously provided by the guests of the hotel. I brought them every morning some crumbs and other tidbits left over from breakfast. In the park I noticed some other, smaller birds, probably some song birds recently returned, busily making their nests. The songs of all these birds resounded all over the park, and the characteristic twittering of blackbirds was particularly noticeable in the early dusk.

February is traditionally the month of love and lovers, the month when young (and not only young) people observe St. Valentine's Day on 14 February. It is an ancient custom among the young people in England and in America to choose a sweetheart, a lover, or a special friend for the ensuing year, and to send a present, usually a card with a special message to the person thus chosen. The custom has been observed in England since the mid-fifteenth century, but its origin is obscure. There is a rural tradition that birds choose their mates on St. Valentine's Day. The custom has been frequently mentioned in English literature, from the times of Chaucer and Shakespeare down to Hardy.

> *And smale fowles maken melodye,*
> *that slepen all the night with open ye,*
> *so priketh hem nature in her corages.*
> And little birds make melody
> sleeping all the night with open eye
> so nature excites them in their feelings.

This is a well-known passage from the Prologue to Chaucer's Canterbury Tales, which I still remember from my student days. So, February is a month which puts me in a special, wistful and restless mood, when I feel like walking out most of the day, and various fragments of poetry, read and remembered long ago, float through my mind.

O spring, o time of love, how sadly
Your advent swamps me in its flood.
And in my soul, o spring, how madly
Your presence aches, and in my blood.

Pushkin's lovely lines from *Eugene Onegin* sound much sweeter and better in Russian, faithfully reflecting our mood and our feelings at that time of the year.

"I must tell you about a most extraordinary thing", said the Austrian lady, who every winter comes from Vienna to Opatija at the same time as we do.

"Imagine, I have seen two swans swimming in the bay of Volosko, two real swans. They appear to be quite tame and accepted bread from some children".

How extraordinary, indeed, I thought. And I felt quite excited at the news and wondered whether I should be lucky enough to see those strange birds, too. As I thought about them I remembered that swans usually favour lakes and rivers, I have never heard of them swimming in the sea. But, who knows ? The story of Andersen's wild swans came to my mind. Many years ago, while Father was still alive, we spent several winters in Primošten, a small fishing village, and one February morning I happen to see a flock of wild swans flying over our village. They circled for a moment as if they were deliberating whether to make a stop there, but then in a matter of seconds they disappeared in the distance, leaving me looking after them in a state of amazement. It was the only time that I have seen those beautiful, mighty birds. An unforgetable experience.

The news about the two swans captured not only my imagination, but they soon became the talk of our little community. Everybody I met seemed to have seen them, everybody except me, in spite of my repeated efforts to do so. I went to the harbour of Volosko, where the swans were reported to have been seen, and tried to talk to some fishermen, local people. They all claimed that they had seen the swans both swimming in Volosko, tame enough to accept bread from the delighted children, and as far away as the Belvedere hotel, where my sister and I were staying. It was so provoking to know that they had been so close to me and yet I had failed to see them.

The following day I heard that their picture, taken by some young person from Volosko, had appeared in the local paper. I tried to get hold of that paper through our chambermaid, but though she promised she would bring it, she always forgot to do so. Even the hairdresser, who came to the hotel to do my sister's hair, told us that her son was able to photograph them. Those swans set my imagination racing. There must have been some serious reason, thought I, for those noble, wild creatures to have taken refuge so close to humans. One of them must have been in some kind of trouble to make her (for some reason I was convinced that it was a female) drop out of the flock with which they were flying to the north. I was moved at the thought that her companion stayed by her side at that critical moment. I remembered that many birds live in pairs, for life, until "death does them part" , and are therefore more constant and loyal than we humans are.

I was very unhappy that I did not succeed in seeing them. I walked about looking for them with my head full of fragments of the music from Swan's Lake, and bits of poetry with swans figuring in them.

> Yes, in that spring-time, in low-lying
> secluded vales, where swans were crying,
> by waters that were still and clear
> for the first time the Muse came near.

Thus Pushkin again. A swan is a poet's bird, and a symbol of his loneliness and reclusion.

A couple of days had gone by, the swans remaining still mysteriously elusive to me. Then the weather changed again. It became very cold. I did not hear the swans being much talked about. They had, apparently, flown away. I wondered how they fared in that cold weather.

One morning when I was waiting my turn in a little grocer's shop in Volosko, the woman-assistant with whom I always exchanged a few friendly phrases, addressed me:

"Do you remember the swans we talked about the other day ?

It appears that they had escaped from a private owner in Punat, on the island of Krk".

I did not receive this banal explanation without offering some resistance and expressing my doubts:

"How can that be ? And how did their owner learn of their whereabouts"?

"Simply, from the papers where there was their picture".

I went back to the hotel in a dejected mood. All my romantic notions about the two swans were shattered to pieces. They were not wild swans after all. And nobody was in trouble. They were tame birds playing truants. Ah, well.

And yet, on second thought I believe they deserved our sympathy.

"Spring, the sweet spring".

A Strange Companion

Once again, I had come here, for a brief holiday, without my sister this time; she could not stand the journey as she was not feeling well enough. So, after many years, this was the first time that I was alone in Opatija, and this gave my stay quite a new character. When you are alone you make use of your time differently than when you have company. And for this reason you are bound to notice things that otherwise might have passed unnoticed.

Walking by the sea was my principal pastime. The weather being fine, I spent the greater part of the day outside, an activity other visitors engaged in, too. Both domestic and foreign visitors were not so numerous as in previous years, no doubt because of the developing political and economic crisis in our country. The time of great changes seemed to have arrived.

At this time of year most visitors to Opatija are elderly people, who come here because the prices are more affordable than during the tourist season. They come from all parts of our country. Opatija has a great many attractions, the vicinity of Trieste not being among the least. For to go shopping in Trieste and come back with some bargains has become a matter of personal prestige, even long after similar goods could be purchased in our country as well. At the same time some Italian tourists come over here to take advantage of cheaper food products, or like some of their pensioners to spend a winter holiday in our hotels, which are less expensive than their old peoples homes. I often encounter them, walking in small groups like a flock of gay sparrows. And they resemble them because they are never silent. They constantly chatter, laugh, and occasionally sing popular Neapolitan tunes. They are true, carefree Mediterraneans.

But there were quite a few solitary walkers, and others who sat alone on benches looking absentmindedly at the blue, sparkling sea. They were left to themselves and their own thoughts either by choice or because they had nobody to keep them company.

After one such solitary walk, I returned to the park of our hotel, Belvedere, to find a bench where I could enjoy sitting in the mild February sunshine. The bench I was looking for was in a quiet and remote corner of the park, on a small terrace of the annex, which at this time of the year was closed down. Few guests knew of this secluded spot and as a consequence I came to consider it my private refuge.

This terrace offered a lovely view of Quarnero Bay and the island of Cres, glimmering like a mirage in the blue haze. Ancient pine trees and other Mediterranean shubbery protected my little shelter, while the bare and twisted branches of an old oak tree struck a somewhat discordant note in this pastoral environment.

I was looking forward to resting in my hidden haven. But, when I climed a few steps leading to the terrace I became aware that I would not be alone there. Well protected behind an earthenware vase in which grew a huge oleander, an old woman was sitting on my bench. She was obviously not one of the hotel guests but rather one of the townsfalk, many of whom were in the habit of passing through the hotel park. Her dress was modest but neat; instead of shoes, she wore warm felt slippers, and a strange-looking woolen hat that was too small to cover all of her white hair. As soon as she noticed me, she, with a sweet and polite smile, began to make room for me on the bench. At the same time she was making signs to me to keep quiet, pointing to something under the bench. I looked in that direction but all I could see were the bread crumbs she had left there.

"There is a small birdie here", she said to me in a whisper. "It comes here every day to feed. It is so pretty with yellow feathers round its neck". As she said that, she pointed to her neck to show what she meant. "But you must keep quiet for it to show up".

While I kept my gaze upon the crumbs expecting the appearance of the marvelous birdie, the old woman called it "ptiček". she must have quietly got up and left the bench.

for when I next looked toward her, I found that she was not there any more. And so I was left alone on the bench.

I sat there, oblivious of the time, greatly enjoying the beauty and the quiet. As I listened and watched, I took great delight in everything around me. From time to time the wind gently sighed through the branches of the pine trees. I could observe some small winged creatures fluttering around a bush that had only recently begun to blossom. Among them I detected first busy bees, but also the annoying flies. It was a whole and separate world of tiny creatures coexisting with our human worlds, without either being conscious of the other. It felt good for a brief moment to come closer to that other world. The voices of the strollers walking along the beach a short distance away reached me from time to time. They sounded unreal and appeared to me jarring and too loud, as they interrupted the peace of the flora and fauna around me.

All of a sudden I became aware that I was no longer alone. At the lower bar of the metal balustrade of the terrace stood the small bird the old woman was talking about. It was truly beautiful. With its tiny legs firmly gripping the bar it was expectantly looking at me with its round, black eyes. Every now and then it turned its head this way and that way. We were silently examining each other, and this mute exchange lasted for a few minutes. I admired the bird, but I did not know what it thought of me. It was certain that it was not afraid of me. It appeared to me that we existed alone in separate worlds of our own. Finally, the "ptiček" put end to this mutual examination, and as if it had made up its mind about me, it hopped down among the crumbs that the old woman had left there, and slowly and delicately it began to pick them up. Now, I could see it a little better. Its back was of brown-grey colour, while its breast was almost white. Its beak was small, but very sharp, and it used it with great dexterity to pick up the crumbs. I know hardly anything about birds, but I think it might have belonged to the species of garden warblers (Sylvidae); this information I found in an old book on birds that used to belong to my daughter when she was a student.

I remembered that the old woman told me that this bird liked to be talked to, and I decided to put her statement to the test. I could not say how much the birdie liked it, but it did not appear frightened of my voice. I am more inclined to think that it remained indifferent to it, completely absorbed in picking up of the crumbs. When it was sufficiently fed it flitted away to the nearby bush and disappeared there. It had gone back to its proper world, and, I, too, very pleased with my new acquaintance, decided to return to the hotel, back to the human world to which I belonged.

My brief stay in Opatija was drawing to an end. The day I was to leave I was obliged to get up very early in order to catch the bus for the airport, which is on the island of Krk. It was before 6 o'clock in the morning when I passed through the completely deserted park of our hotel. Daylight was just beginning to break, but the old park was alive and full of bird twitterings. In my thoughts I was taking leave of this charming place, so dear to me, and of my little birdie, which was certainly no longer asleep.

An unpleasant surprise awaited me at the airport. On such a sunny and clear morning it was difficult to believe that our flight had to be delayed because of the dense fog at the Surčin airport in Belgrade. A more likely reason was that our plane had been pinched to fly some foreign tourists, a practice adopted by the JAT company for extra revenue. So, all the passengers, bitterly disappointed, were returned to Opatija, where at the JAT office we were told that our flight was scheduled for 9 o'clock that evening. An unpleasant memory is associated with this episode. I remember how unfriendly and rude the bus driver of the airport bus was. It was a direct flight so all the passengers were from Belgrade, and no doubt Serbs. The bus driver did not hide his dislike of Serbs, which he demonstrated in a most unfriendly way. When we were returned from the airport for the second time, he stopped at the Rijeka railway station and told us that he would not take us any farther, and that we should now take care of ourselves. It was a completely arbitrary decision, for the bus always left from and returned to Opatija, because of the passengers. This was a small but still telling illustration of what many people in Croatia felt about Serbs.

As we had all given notice to our hotels, it meant spending a whole day in the street, almost 12 hours, waiting for our flight. I decided to go for a walk before lunch, and then to return to the park of my hotel to rest a little on the bench on the secluded terrace.

The bench was fortunately unoccupied. It was the time of the day when few people remain outside. The calm of the early afternoon reigned over the whole place. Tired after a long walk, I stretched out on the bench. Once more I immersed myself in the magic of the other, parallel world of the quiet and of the crawling and winged creatures. I tried to fall asleep, but the bench was too hard, and the sun was too hot. I began to watch the flight of restless and busy bees, and of some other winged insects. The ants were apparently aimlessly running to and fro on the big earthenware vase, on some mysterious errands. Then, all of a sudden, I noticed my birdie. Almost noiselessly it had alighted upon the same spot and began to look at me with some curiosity, turning its head this way and that. It appeared to be not quite pleased with something. I immediately guessed what annoyed it. There was not a single bread crumb on the terrace, and I had nothing to offer it. The bird stood there on its skinny legs that were somewhat astride a while longer still hoping some food might be coming its way, then looking disappointed, it turned around and flew away.

Fare thee well, my little companion, it is to you I dedicate this little story.

It was in February of 1991, and I did not know that it would be a farewell to Opatija, too. For only a couple of months later Yugoslavia was plunged into a civil war, and these parts of my former homeland had become a foreign country to me, which I would visit as a foreign tourist.

Belgrade, Kalemagdan Fort, confluence of the Sava and the Danube

Belgrade

As previously arranged, we were picked up from our Hotel in Budapest by the owner of a private minibus, which was to take us to Belgrade. There were 9 people, including a small boy of 3 years of age, crammed in the bus, most of them from the USA, and a few from Canada. The luggage area was packed to capacity with enormous trunks and bags. All of the passengers had close relatives in Belgrade and were bringing things that were either scarce or else too expensive to buy there, because of the embargo imposed upon Serbia two years ago.

Our bus was one of a multitude of all sorts of vehicles, coming from different parts of Europe and former Yugoslavia. Their number slowed the customs and passport procedures, resulting in hours of waiting. I noticed a long line of

Belgrade, Kalemagdan Fort

lorries with Slovenian registration – the laws of business have obviously proved stronger than those of politics, and they find the way to circumvent embargo barriers. From bits of conversation heard during the frequent stops I could get a feeling of general atmosphere and frame of mind of our people. In spite of much criticism of the government's policy they were all optimistic about the future of Serbia, making light of the hardship the embargo had had on their lives and the economy of the country.

Belgrade, the Moskva Hotel on Terazije

It was late in the afternoon when we reached Belgrade, and it was already evening when first my daughter and then I were brought to the door of the friends each of us was to stay with. Rina remained in Birčaninova with Vukosava Kojen, an old friend of mine, and I was taken to Kosovska 5, the former home of my sister.

I remembered my arrival in Belgrade nearly thirty years ago, when on a cold January morning I stepped down on the icebound platform of Belgrade station. I remembered how struck I was by the odd sights of the "Šiptars", the ethnic Albanians, who invaded Belgrade in search for work. Dressed in a characteristic and strange mixture of their ethnic costumes and the city garb, they stood in sharp contrast to other passers-by in the streets. Each carried a small axe undrer the arm -a sign of recognition and a symbol of their

Belgrade, fountain in Knez Mihailova Street

occupation. They were experts in chopping wood, which they then carried and stored in cellars. That was one of the lasting impressions I received when in 1964 I moved from Zagreb to Belgrade. I realized that I had travelled far into the east. The difference between these two cities was manifest in many other ways. To take only the names of the streets and other parts in each of them. In Zagreb I discovered such names as *Jagodnjak* – Strawberry Lane, *Ružićnjak* – Briarwood Lane, *Paunovac* – Peacock Lane, *Svibovac* – Dogwood Lane, *Mlinarska cesta* – Miller's Road, to mention but a few. The toponyms in Belgrade told us a different story. They kept and revealed the secrets of an other, different past. When I came to Belgrade I was greatly amused and puzzled by the names of some parts of the town. For a long time I could not make sense of the name Palilula, given to a community in Belgrade, until one day I learnt that during the Turkish rule Christian Raya were allowed to smoke,"to light their pipes", only in an area strictly designated to them. To this day other bigger towns in Serbia have their Palilulas,too. It was difficult to believe that Tašmajdan, one of the biggest and most beautiful parks right in the center of the town, was once a quarry - for that is what the name means. Of a more poetic character was the word Bulbulder, designating an area in Belgrade where nightingales sang by the brook . They apparently still sing there in spite of the fact that the original brook was long transformed into a public fountain. And what to think of Rospi ćuprija ? The word rospija was used by Turks to refer to a prostitute, and according to an interpretation it was from that bridge that women of bad reputation were pushed into the water. Such memories crossed my mind as I looked at the familiar streets from our bus.

At first glance Belgrade looked little changed since I left it two years before. I was surprised at the lively traffic despite the restrictions and the short supply of gas. I remembered the groups of private cars we had noticed on each side of the road leading to Belgrade. They belonged to the people who crossed over to Hungary only to fill their tanks with gas, which they later sold in Belgrade for a good price.

I was equally surprised to see the shop windows displaying a variety of goods, even imported luxury goods, such as foreign drinks and spirits, cosmetics, tobacco, etc. From what I had heard and read in the letters from my friends from Belgrade, I had thought that I would find that they were in need of the most basic things. I was, therefore, greatly embarassed with the utilitarean and practical presents that I had brought them, like tooth paste, tea,coffee, stockings etc. The presents were received with much grace, and if my friends were surprised and disappointed by them, they did not let me feel it. However, they told me that the temporary scarcity of provisions and empty supermarkets was actually an artifice devised by shopkeepers to make greater profits during the period of inflation. I was equally impressed by the good spirits of all the friends I visited during my short stay. Nobody complained, so that I was left with the impression that things had somehow taken a turn for the better. This was definitely confirmed by the fact that recently the Dinar had been devalued and at the time we were in Belgrade 1 Dinar was worth 1 DM. A true miracle.

It felt strange to stay as a guest in the flat and the house which until recently had belonged to my sister, and in which I had lived with her for the previous twenty years. It was her death that prompted me to immigrate to America, to join my daughter and my grandchildren there, the only family I was left with.

The actual reason for my visit to Belgrade was to see if it would be possible to secure the payment of my pension, which had not been forwarded to me since I had left Belgrade. Nothing, of course, could be done for the country had no hard currency to spare, and so I gave the power of attorney to my lawyer to receive it on my behalf until further notice. Likewise, the money (Dollars and D.M.) I had in a bank account in Belgrade existed also on paper only. In reality the money had been spent long ago by the state, and God knows when and if it will ever be returned. During my stay I had another unpleasant surprise. I learnt from an acquaintance that his sister had bought the flat in which she was staying for an insignificant sum of money, paid in D.M. What was interesting about it is the fact that the flat was private property that had been nationalized by the Partisans when they came to power after the war. When the Milošević government succeeded them nationalized property became state property, and a year or so before I left, there was much talk that the new government would return former private property to the original owners. They had done something to that effect only with peasant land and property, but nothing at all with the houses and other objects in urban areas. After my sister's death I inherited the flat in which we had lived as well as, legally at least and if only on paper, the house on Kosovska 5, in which we stayed. And now, I learnt that the state had robbed us twice, first when the property had been nationalized, and now again, when it sold these flats and houses before they would have to return them to their legal owners. However, all this is beside the point, I mention it only to illustrate what can happen to people who live under regimes like those we have had and still have.

I also went to the cemetery to see the family graves. Both father and mother are buried here, and my sister Branka lies with the rest of the Šondas in their family vault. When I was getting ready to immigrate to the USA I had an agreement with a friend of mine, a Russian lady, that she would look after my dead family, and in return I transferred to her the legal right to be buried in my family vault, where I believed I would lie one day next to my parents. Destiny has decreed America for my last resting place. This arrangement was satisfactory for both of us, for to find a place to be buried in this Belgrade cemetery was next to impossible, and if at all then at a very high price. And I was happy that at least for the time being somebody would take care of the graves I had left in Belgrade. I often think that I had moved to Belgrade only to bury one after the other, my mother, my father and finally my sister. It was my lot to close the door of both houses.

Belgrade, St. Mark's church on Tašmajdan

Of Snails and Men

I also went to Tašmajdan, a park in the vicinity of Kosovska, where I had often walked our dachshund Dikole. Taš-majdan was a grave-yard in the past century, way out of the town; today it is one of the biggest parks right in the centre of town. From the balconies of our flat in Kosovska we could hear the bells and see the round domes of St.Mark's church. Close to it stands the small Russian church I occasionally attended. Its whitewashed walls and small cupola painted in intense blue are so unlike the stately architecture of St.Mark's, which is built all in stone, a modern, less impressive version of the medieval Gračanica in Serbo-Byzantine style.

When you frequently take your dog to the same park sooner or later you become familiar with other regular visitors there. Any newcomer, of course, is immediately noticed and viewed with curiosity and suspicion. It was, therefore, with surprise and resentment that upon arriving in the park one fine, crisp April morning, I noticed two strange figures busily looking for something under the bushes that grew in one corner of the park. They were two gypsies - a thin, old woman with a cigarette in the corner of her mouth, and a very young girl carrying a big cloth bag over her shoulders. They both wore their traditional gayly coloured calico dresses; their rather faded head scarves and well worn shoes already at first glance made it clear that they did not belong in this urban setting, to which they made frequent but always temporary visits.

I could not make out what they were doing, and decided to ask them. The old woman reluctantly turned her head up, took a good look at me, and then gave this laconic answer:

"Collecting snails".

"Snails ?", I said very much astonished while the two gypsies went on with their work, completely ignoring my presence. They deftly detected and picked up lovely, big snails, which with their delicate, white shells had crawled all over the fresh, morning grass.

My astonishment gave place to indignation. Ever since my childhood I had felt a special fascination for snails. It is not that I had seen them often, but for some reason the ones I had seen or read about had stuck in my memory. I remember how I had first, as a small girl, discovered those strange creatures crawling across the path of aunt Alka's garden in Travnik leaving intricate and iridescent marks behind them. I was intrigued by those creatures which carried their homes on their back and which had their eyes on the top of their horns. All very strange. As children we used to sing a little song to induce a snail to stretch out its horns:

Pusti pužu roge van,
Da ti kuću ne prodam…
Let your horns come out, snail,
Or else I'll sell your house…

Snails seem to have made an impression on some writers, too, and found a permanent place in their works. I, at least, remember the snail living in the house of the Blue Fairy in the story about Pinocchio. And who does not remember the couple of old and distinguished snails that lived in an overgrown garden in Hans Christian Anderson's story the Happy Family ? Their main preocupation was to find a bride for their son. Their only regret was that they had not followed the destiny of their predecessors, who were all in turn boiled and brought to the table on a silver platter. They thought that this would be a supreme sign of distinction they could hope to achieve in their lifetime.

Meanwhile the two gypsies went on very diligently and apparently very successfully with their task. But I wanted to find out what destiny had in store for these snails from Tašmajdan.

"And what will you do with them ?"

The old woman paused for a moment, perhaps to rest a little, and then she said:

"Take them to a man who buys them. He is paying well - one thousand dinars for a kilo. He sends them, I think, to France and Italy."

As I watched them leaving the park with a bagful of snails, another picture came back to my mind. It was a cold November morning, and I was walking in one of the streets in the residential part of Belgrade, when I noticed a small fire burning at the corner of a small square. Two young gypsies, traditional street cleaners in our town, with brooms in their hands stood gazing at the fire improvised with a few sticks and dry leaves. When I came quite close I could see that several slices of tomatoes and green peppers together with a couple of live snails were grilled on a piece of old sheet metal, probably found in the street and ingeniously used as a pan.

Those two gypsy women put me in the mood to think of their kin, the last nomads of our time, and discrete observers of our life and customs. Living on the fringe of society gypsies have always been quick to find out what was in demand at a particular moment and knew how to cater to such needs, and turn it to their advantage. They are very adaptable, but at the same time they remain aloof, jealously guarding their freedom and independence.

My earliest memories of these people take me back to the days when as children we were threatened into beleaving in "keribaba", an imaginary old gypsy woman, who came with her bag to take away naughty children. Despite the fact that we had never seen the "keribaba", we believed in her, for we had seen gypsy women going from door to door begging or trying to tell fortunes from one's palms or from their cards in order to earn some money. Later, I remember young gypsy girls coming to our town on Lazarus' Saturday and on St.George's Day. St. George's Day was our family's patron saint, and we observed his day on the 6th of May. This holiday was associated with all kinds of ancient rituals and customs observed not only by Orthodox people but also by Catholics and Moslems, which bears witness to the antiquity and authenticity of those customs. Regardless of their religion people in our town, Tuzla, would go on outings into the nature on that May morning to celebrate the day, making merry and singing traditional songs to the accompaniment of accordion. Such an outing was in fact a celebration of the beginning of a new cycle of vegetation. Gypsies always observed that holiday. They knew the families whose patron saint it was, and dressed in dark if somewhat shabby suits, with a posy of lilies-of-the-valley in their buttonholes, they would turn up at our door and begin to play some of the songs traditionally associated with that holiday. With them usually came several young gypsy girls, "dodole", to sing and perform a dance. At the first sound of their violins, members of the family, usually children, would rush to the door to listen to their music, and to watch the dance performed by the dodole, adorned with gay ribbons and handkerchiefs. At the time it was a common enough sight, but today it appears to me as a scene from a folk tale. Dodole, are actually girls who sing for rain, as rainmakers, they represent the remnants of a very old custom, whose rites invoked and ensured rain and fertility. At the time when my sister and I watched them perform that dance and sing that old song, perhaps of a magic character, nobody was aware any longer of its meaning:

Ova kuća bogata,
Pet stotina dukata,
(This is a rich house,
Worth five hundred ducats…)

The traditional song that used to be sung to invoke the rain runs as follows:

Naša doda Boga moli,
Da udari rosna kiša,
Mi idemo preko sela,
A oblaci preko neba,
A mi brže, oblak brže,
Oblaci nas pretekoše,
Žito, vino porosiše,
I tri pera kukuruza,
Oj, dodo,dodole...
(Our doda begs of God,
To give us heavy dewy rain,
We are going across the field
The clouds are rushing across the sky,
We quicken up our step, and so do the clouds,
But the clouds overtook us
And they sprinkled the wheat and vineyards,
And three stalks of the maize,
Oy, dodo, dodole...)

In former days peasant girls decked with green leaves would go around from house to house, and sing this song, which was intended to invoke the rain, but today all that has remained of this custom is an expression to describe a tastelessly dressed woman. We say that she looks "like a dodola".

Meanwhile, mother would come out to offer them some refreshments, and to receive their good wishes for the holiday, and to give them some money.

I have a fond and nostalgic recollection of Dr.Bučić, my father's colleague, who used to come on St.George's Day morning with a bouquet of lilies-of-the-valley to greet our mother with a little song traditionally sung on that day:

Djurdjevska kišica sitno rosila,
Djevojka kišobran svilen nosila,
Djurdjevska kišice, man'se cure te,
Već ti padaj sad na usjeve...
(St.George's rain was gently falling,
A young girl with a silk umbrella was walking,
St.George's rain, leave that girl alone,
And apply yourself to the wheat fields...)

A less attractive picture then came to my mind – a picture I have often seen in the streets of Belgrade. A group of gypsies leading by a chain an old, ragged bear, which obediently followed them. From time to time they would stop at a promising spot and when the first sounds of the flute and the monotonous beating of the drum could be heard, the bear would rear itself on its hind legs to perform its pathetic dance. The amused passers-by and other spectators from nearby windows generously threw coins into the readily available hat or tambourine. Such a sight could often be seen on the 29th of November, the official holiday of former Yugoslavia. In the gloomy, cold atmosphere of November, they appeared to me like anachronistic relics of a distant, barbaric past. Hardly any better than the bear baiting from Elizabethan times, when similar, and even more cruel and revolting sights served to entertain the enlightened citizens of London.

As time passed people began to recover from the Second World war and so their needs and requirements began to change too. With great speed and readiness gypsies realized what was in demand in this new situation and found ways to meet it. And so, all of a sudden the streets of Belgrade were often visited by gypsy dealers who offered for sale old oil lamps,clocks of all shapes and origin, and looking-glasses with golden frames. They have quickly realized that they could make good money selling such status symbols to the members of the newly formed bourgeois class. These gypsy antique dealers offered old icons, often of great value and beauty, forsaken by the younger generation. I was able to admire an authentic Louis XVI chest-of-drawers in the home of one of my friends, also purchased from gypsies. They would drag such a large piece of furniture into a building entrence and then, standing at the entrance gate, would estimate who among the passers-by might be a likely buyer before inviting him to come in and have a look at their treasure. What interesting and unconventional antique shops they improvised in this manner. I often wondered where they discovered all these things, very likely in the attics of small towns in Vojvodina, or even as far away as Hungary, whose inhabitants had access to all the refined products of Central European bourgeois culture. Strange are the ways followed by these modern nomads. Many of them still travel with their tents drawn by horses, but the number using modern means of transportation is ever greater, many of them driving cars bought, of course, second-hand. Without a permanent profession and dwelling, the gypsies are obliged, more so than the rest of us, to use their wits. Without the worries that beset the members of the consumer society they, careless and free, travel like snails carrying their homes with them.

A Family Museum

"Well, aren't we going to see the calves as well ?", asked our host Dule. He was a driver in the Cobex firm where my sister's husband used to work. Dule often drove him on business trips even as far as Germany and Italy. After his death my sister occasionally asked Dule to drive us in her car on various excursions, when she did not feel like driving such long distances. One year when my grandchildren came from America to spend the summer with us, Dule drove us all the way to Cavtat, on the Adriatic coast.

Dule was born in Blaznava, a small village in the heart of Šumadija, not far from Topola. He often invited us to come and be his guests on a Sunday to spend a day in his village. We did not know how beautiful this region was and how charming his little village of Blaznava was. It is reached via Topola and Mladenovac taking a road which leads through a gentle and green countryside, full of orchards, fields and meadows streaked with groves of trees. In times past, in the Middle Ages and later, here stood dense almost impassable forests, which have given the name of Šumadija -Woodland- to this part of Serbia as is witnessed in travel-records written by travelers from Western Europe and also by Evliya Ćelebiya, the tireless traveler from the East.

In Šatornja Donja, a small village before Blaznava, we had lunch in a rather shabby roadside inn with several lorries parked in front of it. Lorry drivers have the reputation of knowing where food is good, and in this firm belief we ordered our lunch from a young mustached and gloomy innkeeper. To our great disappointment neither the cottage cheese with "pogača" (unleavened bread), the traditional hors d'oeuvre in these parts, nor the cold roast lamb proved to be what we expected. Perhaps lorry drivers have become less discriminating, or perhaps we expecterd too much.

After Šatornja Donja, we left the good asphalt road and set off for Blaznava on a very bad and steep country road, which was difficult to negotiate even with our sturdy and trusty Volks-wagen. Luckily, we did not encounter any other vehicles; the only other travelers were an occasional pedestrian, and flocks of sheep.

We stopped in front of a big wooden gate of old-fashioned style with a saddle roof. Several wreaths made from some plants and country flowers decked the gate. They had been hanging there wilted and dried since St.George's Day, when young peasant girls went out into the fields and forests to pick flowers and make wreaths which they then place on the house doors and windows and gates. Dule's brother, who also was only on a day visit to his old home in Blaznava, told us that when he was a youth he and his mates spent a whole night in the woods,and in this manner they greeted the arrival of St.George's Day. The wreaths were an ancient custom, but he was not able to tell us its meaning. It is, perhaps, the relic of a belief in the magic power of various plants and flowers to protect man and cattle from the evil eye.

Our host gave us a tour of his home. The old family house stood in the middle of a large yard that looked almost like a garden. We were surprised to see every corner of it covered by lush, fresh grass, it was clear that there was nobody there to mow it. The old house was built on a slope so that its lower part served as a cellar for the storage of several large barrels. In times past they were full of wine from their vine-yards. This region is excellent for wine growing and yields the famous wines from Oplenac. Both Dule and his brother had abandoned their land and village and moved into the town, Dule to become a driver, his brother to become a worker in the chamotte factory in Arandjelovac. The vineyard, which requires a lot of hard work, has fallen into complete neglect since the death of their parents. Today, they distill plum brandy because plums are much easier to cultivate. The house appeared already at first glance uninhabited. It was obvious that nobody lived there, the front window panes were all broken - an easy target for the village boys and the air guns, they aimed at the turtledoves which had begun to make their nests in this abandoned house. Three long and flat stones, hauled up from the river Jošanica, were ingeniously fashioned into the steps leading to a small, quite empty kitchen. From there you could enter other two rooms provided with beds, one for the parents, the other for the children. Above the beds several family photos hung on the walls. Their parents' wedding picture, sons doing their military service, a few icons - cheap paper reproductions. From the threshold, which was a little raised so that you could sit on it, you had a view of other parts of the courtyard. A small wooden house without windows, like something out of a Russian folk tale, stood on the right side. Its walls were made of horizontal planks separated by small cracks to admit some light. This was the "vayat" in which the newly-weds spend their first night all by themselves; only later on they join the rest of the family in the house. This strange house is no longer in use; instead it serves as a convenient storeroom for all sorts of unnecessary things. A small squat house on the left, once a summer kitchen, was left to fall apart a long time ago. It still had two massive wooden chests that could hold more than 100 kg of flour. Between these two houses stood a well, built of bricks with a wooden roof to protect its clean and always cool water. Water was drawn by means of a winch with a simple bucket hanging from an iron chain. The well, too, was decorated with wreaths and flowers, which had long been dead and wilted. I was told that they are never removed but are left to stand there until they fall off. Periwinkle grew in profusion all around the well and its blue flowers were reminiscent of a graveyard, an association sustained by the general sense of desolation and waste around us. As in the story of the Sleeping Beauty everything was overgrown with thick grass; wild vine spread its tentacles across the roof of the old house, and the place seemed to have fallen into a profound sleep.

There were other flowers there, too - white and red peonies, carnations, a marshmallow bush and an old and solitary rose that had grown into a real tree. The rose tree in Dule's garden must have been very old, for it was dotted with numerous scars left by former masters when they pruned it. There was also a shady linden tree with a small bench under it, a comfortable place to rest on a hot summer day. Everything showed signs of long and loving care once bestowed upon this piece of land. Dule told us, not without pride, that his family had lived here for over 150 years. He left for last his new house, built on the highest point of the orchard, and partly hidden by it. Everything in this house was new, banal, impersonal and mass-produced. In a small room upstairs Dule showed us what he had collected and preserved from their old family house.

"When I finally get to repair our old house, I intend to use these things to arrange a family museum there", he told us while we looked at various objects coming from the old household spread without any order on the floor of the room. All kinds of wooden vessels, whose names were unknown to me, and which were used for milking the cow, for skimming milk and making cheese, stood side by side with distaffs, spindles, and other implements necessary for spinning wool. From among the kitchen utensils I liked best a big wooden "lopar", a scoop used to place bread into the oven and to take it out. A wooden yoke, in which they harnessed their oxen, has also found its resting place here. Few people plow their fields with a plow and oxen nowadays. The yoke was painted bright red, a custom in these parts, and even today you occasionally encounter an oxen cart painted vivid red and adorned with floral patterns.

We sat down to rest at a small wooden table that Dule and his brother had placed in the garden for us. We were under the spell of this lovely May day and of nature resplendend in its spring time. The rustling of the wind in the branches of the linden tree and lilac bushes, the singing of birds, the cackling of hens and the crowing of the cock from the neighbourhood created an atmosphere of wellbeing. We felt in harmony with our environment. Dule left us to mow the grass while we talked with his brother. We heard that his two daughters were students in Belgrade, one studying English, the other mathematics. And so, his children will become city dwellers, and who knows what they will gain and what they will lose in the process. Their father still stands with one foot in the village, and the other in the town.

After World War II, he told us, a great many people from their village left for America, for Chicago. It was on the whole a political emigration, after the advent of communism, following the earlier, economic emigration. People here have been, and have probably remained, loyal to the king and the dynasty. During the war they had fought on the side of Draža Mihailović. Dule told a little anecdote from which it will be easy to see on whose side their sympathies lay.

A peasant was plowing his field with a plow and a horse. Marshal Tito came along and much surprised at what he saw, he asked the peasant:

"Why do you, comrade, plow your field with a plow ? Why don't you have a tractor like other people in our country ? Don't you remember how we fought together to achieve this ?"

The peasant looked at him for a while, and then replied:

"Dear me, Dražo, what has become of you? You have changed so much that I would never have recognized you".

We were sipping the wine Dule's brother had brought from their cellar. A small girl, dressed in city fashion like all the village children now are, came to greet us and to bring her neighbours some gifts of food sent by her mother - an old custom meant to promote good relation between neighbours. On a plate she has brought several fresh and a few painted eggs from Easter, which fell very late this year.

It was so nice to sit in the mild spring sunshine that we did not notice that the sun had already passed the greater part of its daily path. Dule had put away his scythe and came to join us, pleased to have mown the grass round his new house.

"Well, then, aren't we going to see the calves?"he asked us.

We set out all together along a narrow and very neglected country lane to see the calves of čiča Raka, which Dule was mentioning. The village we were passing through looked very pleasant with houses in the midst of orchards.

Čiča Raka's house was larger and much older than Dule's family house; it was a good example of village architecture from Šumadija. Its roof was covered with "ćeramida", tiles of a special triangular shape, so that they could be arranged in a dovetail fashion. We found the old man in the stable feeding his calves. We were overwhelmed by the peculiar and pleasant smell, a mixture of hay and manure, which I remembered from my childhood. Three calves and two young cows, well groomed and well fed, looked indifferently at us with their large, shiny eyes. Čiča Raka, tiny and very thin, and already completely greyhaired, gave us a warm and confused welcome. A few months ago he had lost his wife, baba, as Dule and his brother called her, and since her death čiča Raka had been living all by himself. He took care of himself and of his cattle, but what we could conclude at first glance was that he cared best for his cattle. When they come to their village,Dule and his brother prepare some warm food to take to čiča Raka, who is not adept at cooking, for his baba seems to have spoiled him. She must have been a great housekeeper. "Nobody knew how to pickle cabbage as she did", said Dule knowingly with a deep sigh. We asked cica Raka to show us his house, which he did with good grace. We first entered an area from which several doors led to other rooms. He opened the door of their bedroom. Several wooden beds were lined up against the walls, with cushions and thick woolen home-made rugs scattered in disorder over them. An unpleasant, acrid and sour smell emanated from those unaired beddings. Here, too, we could see family photos and cheap icons displayed on the walls. He took us then to the next room, which turned out to be a very large and dark kitchen. One glance was enough to see that this was the central, the most important area in the whole house, where his wife had spent most of her time.

But now, it all looked dead and desolate. Unlike the floor in the other rooms, here the floor was of dirt, uneven in certain places. On the right was a large fire place, where in former days an ox could be roasted. Sunk in deep ashes lay several earthenware vessels and some round iron covers used for baking bread. A big tin stove, called a 'fijaker', all black and shiny, stood close by the fire place. Dule told us that it was custom-made by their village blacksmith. It was on this 'fijaker' that čiča Raka's baba prepared the savory dishes Dule was sighing for.

A huge, blackened flour chest stood in the opposite corner. We uncovered the lid and saw a mound of flour, well over 100 kg. A tiny silhouette scurried quickly over it and disappeared in a corner of the chest.

A little mouse? Perhaps a whole family lived there? Nobody said a word. We lowered the lid. Small bunches of dried herbs hung on the walls. Perhaps čiča Raka's baba put them to use as a remedy? I remember seeing such bunches of dried herbs in my grandmother's room in Zenica. Several pieces of smoked meat and bacon were hanging on the darkened beams of the ceiling. It had been a well-kept household. A delicious smell of wheat flour and smoke permeated all the kitchen. We walked and spoke very quietly not to disturb the peace that reigned in this area where the spirit of čiča Raka's baba was probably still present. Before we left čiča Raka invited us to take a look at his cellar, and to offer us a drink for a happy journey. It was a sad and altogether neglected cellar. Large barrels stood empty, broken and dried up. Old onions, put away last autumn, had sprouted out of a wicker basket. Even in the darkness of this cellar, green shoots had found their way to light and life.

"I'll give it to the sheep, they like to eat onions" said čiča Raka, taking the basket out of the cellar. He poured out some of his old wine, it was sour, but very strong.

"Excellent wine" we praised it while he smiled modestly. He told us about being in Germany in a prisoners'-of-war camp.

"They treated us well; we were given the same food as their soldiers and officers". Several metal teeth glittered in his mouth, he had lost his own teeth long ago.

"Well, čiča Raka, there is no other way but to marry you again. We shall have to find you some baba, you can't go on living all alone any more. We shall marry you all right", said Dule to cheer him up a little.

We took our leave of čiča Raka, it was time to go home.

"There is nothing worse and sadder than to remain alone in old age, without a wife", said Dule s' brother." I pray to God to take me before my Desanka. It is easier for a woman to remain alone."

Before we left we drank once more some of the sweet and cool water from their well. When we closed the gate we could almost hear the silence filling again every corner of the garden while the old house brooded over past days slowly sinking into a sleep which we had temporarily interrupted.

EPILOGUE

Farewell

THE SAME MINI BUS came to pick us up and take us back to Budapest. At the frontier we had to wait again, and were allowed to leave our bus. I needed to go to the restroom, which was in a separate building near the place we had stopped. An elderly woman was in charge and she requested a "fee" of, I think, 1 DM, which I didn't have, but offered the equivalent in Dollars instead. The woman was adamant, it had to be either a DM, or I wouldn't be able to use the facilities. I was in a ridiculous not to say absurd situation, and I tried to talk sense to her, to no avail. In despair, I decided to go to the nearby restaurant to ask for the same favour, but I was met with an equally unreasonable and unfriendly reception. One of the guests, who got the drift of our argument, offered me the requested DM, and so at long last I was able to make the use of the restrooms. That was an unnecessary nuisance, which left a bad impression of the country and the people. But this was not the end; there was more in store for us. We were not allowed to leave the country before we had paid an "exit tax", of which I had never heard before. It was collected by a very rough and bad-mannered young fellow. What made me mad was not so much the actual amount we were required to pay, but rather the insolent manner in which he treated the passengers. These two episodes, our last contacts with our country, left an unpleasant after-taste. I thought how sad it was that such people come in contact with passengers who are entering or leaving the country, and that such first or last impressions, perhaps unjustly, influence one's opinion of a country and its people.

And thus, we left Yugoslavia, or rather what has remained of it. With a heavy heart I thought of our recent and more distant past, and of the recurrent theme of misunderstandings and rivalries between Serbs and Croats. I grew up in Bosnia, in an atmosphere where religious and ethnic differences were taken for granted, and were respected and tolerated. When in 1939 I married a Croat and came with him to live in Zagreb, as an Orthodox Serb I did not make much of the fact that I had to sign a contract with the Catholic church that all the children from our marriage would be Catholics. At the time it did not matter to me whether they would be Catholic or Orthodox. Soon, however, I was made aware that the differences that distinguished one group from the other had deep roots, resulting from past circumstances beyond our control, and whose consequences were so painfully felt today. Living as a Serb in Croatia during World War Two I had enough opportunity to think about my identity, something which I had never before in my life been particularly aware of. My loyalties were divided between two adverse camps. By marriage I belonged to the one that persecuted and fought the other, to which I belonged by birth. I was constantly oppressed by a sense of guilt for being disloyal either to the one or to the other. For, if I acknowledged the love borne by my husband's family, and the welcome given to me by his friends, I felt I was betraying my unfortunate fellow-countrymen who were brutally persecuted by the Ustaše, the extreme national faction of Croatia.

And now again, for the second time in my life, I am faced with the same dilemma when my former homeland has disintegrated, and where Serbs and Croats are at daggers drawn once again. With all my heart I deplore the demise of Yugoslavia, the only homeland I have known, and which will always remain as such in my heart and mind.

During my brief stay in Zagreb I was all the time aware of an invisible wall separating my friends from myself – it kept us from communicating freely in the way we used to do in the days gone by. The sudden and violent breaking-up of Yugoslavia and the tragic and terrible events that accompanied it have come as a shock to most of us, they have determined the course of our life for years to come. On a more personal, intimate level, the war waged between the Yugoslav Army and the Serbs in Krajina and the Croats has forced each of us to probe the question of our identity - the question I have never before asked myself with such excruciating intensity. And while I think that one's nationality and religion are largelly an accident of birth, I beleive that for that very reason we must honour and respect them. I accept and take pride in the history of the people I was born into, but I do not flinch from feeling the opprobrium for the less glorious and even evil deeds perpertrated by them. When some of my friends in Zagreb said that so far I had not condemned the war in Croatia I resented their calling me to account in this manner. I certainly did not and could not approve of any violent way of settling our problems - our wrongs and grievances - and I think it hardly necessary to proclaim it. All I can say is that I am sorry for all the wrong my fellowcountrymen had done them. But, I reminded them, I could not remember having ever blamed my Croat friends for what the Ustaše were doing during the World War two. And my friends had never, later on, nor today, made any references to or acknowledge those atrocities, let alone express their regrets. I have never reproached them for that. I respected their right to think the way they did, and by the same token I expect them to respect mine. I feel no hatred towards my Croatian friends. I still consider them to be my friends of long standing with whom I had shared good and evil over a long period of time. With great sorrow I think of the alienation and disaffection that has taken place of former trust. I could not feel as comfortable as I did before in this town in which I had spent the best years of my life because of the hatred directed to everything that is called Serb.

Yugoslavia was a bold dream of some of our best people, but the dream could not come true for a number of reasons, the most important, in my opinion, being our past. For centuries Serbs and Croats followed separate and different paths, and were influenced and governed by powers hostile to each other. Differences in their religion and culture have sharply separated Serbs from Croats. And now, with all those bitter memories of recent conflicts and those from World War Two the reconciliation is still too far away to be even considered. I will not live to see it, but I firmly believe and hope that one day it will be possible, when human rights and mutual respect become more important than ethnic and religious differences.

References

(1) *Enciklopedija Jugoslavije Zagreb,* MCMLXXI, Izdanje i naklada Jugoslavenskog leksikografskog zavoda

(2) *The Mountains of Serbia – Travels Through Inland Yugoslavia,* Anne Kindersley, John Murray, Fackal 4, 1976

(3) Lirski Istočnici, *Hatidza Krnjević,* BIGZ Jedinstvo, Beograd 1986

(4) Habeduš Katedralis, *Stari Zagreb,* Impresije iz umirućeg grada, Zagreb, 1932

(5) Martin Dunford and John Holland, *The Real Guide to Yugoslavia,* Prentice Hall, 1985